SO-EIH-232

River Class:

The Way Down

by

Craig Leibfreid

© Craig Leibfreid, 2016

Table of Contents

Chapter 1: A Boom Too Heavy......4

Chapter 2: Sex.......................14

Chapter3: Gauley River Acid.......21

Chapter 4: Archery Season..........38

Chapter 5: Fall Semester............41

Chapter 6: Fasting....................49

Chapter 7: Insanity..................59

Chapter 8: River Class...............64

Chapter 9: Cheat Fest...............66

Chapter 10: Mental Hospital........76

Chapter 11: Trilogy House...........92

Chapter 12: Resurrection...........105

Chapter 13: Spirits..................117

Chapter 14: Peace..................120

Chapter 1: A Boom Too Heavy

7 months after nearly drowning in a kayaking incident at Wonder Falls on the Lower Big Sandy Creek, I returned. First I returned to Morgantown. I had an ounce of reefer and 3 grams of cubensis mushrooms. I planned a fungi trip at the waterfall that nearly claimed my life in the January prior. I spent all summer landscaping and smoking marijuana constantly. The mornings started with some pot-smoke. The work-day passed along with some pot-smoke, and the evening turned to nightfall with some pot-smoke. I became enchanted with delusional mysticism of the natural world. Words and phrases were captured in my mind to ebb the Great Spirit of Creation. The energy and consciousness of the world that surrounded me was studied for months on end with great detail, and I believed there were deep secrets mother nature was hiding from humanity. Those were secrets that could only be revealed in the deepest communions of man and nature, communion that existed in those moments closest to death.

Before returning to Morgantown, I came across a few grams of psychedelic mushrooms. I carried them with me all summer waiting to dive into obscurity when the perfect environment was before me. Sometime in early

August or late July, the time was right. A small gathering in the woods to enjoy the night around a fire was rustled up. The air was warm and the skies were clear. I took my bag of mushrooms along with me for the shear sake of preparation. I had no preconceived concept of what would flow between the people around me, and our natural environment that night. I only knew places and faces. I unrolled my bag of cubensis and pulled out a small cap. I chewed it thoroughly and swallowed. I ate an orange to wash down the dried fungus. I was the only one to trip that night. I sat around the fire next to a friend of mine whom with I shared many long, deep conversations with about nature, spirit, and society. As the psilocybin began to work, I could feel the heat press against my body. I tensed my muscles slightly and absorbed the heat from the flames. A slight sweat began to roll off my body and I embraced it. It seemed like an old Indian trick of the skin walkers to meditate to the sweat. I sat there in trippy meditation listening to the fire crackle and feeling its heat. I stayed hot and sweaty in the cool night air for about three hours and felt my consciousness embracing a natural aura of the field. I controlled my tension and breathing as I sat there drenched in sweat. My consciousness cued upon my friend whom I sat next to. The night went along, and I felt as though I was developing a relationship between my spirit, our spirit, and the spirit around us. The sky turned green, and an aura of mild technicolor emanated, outlining the people whom I felt closest to seated around the fire. At one point I saw a feathered headdress draped over my closest friend, and I had a moment of inspiration. That is, I would eat one mushroom cap every time I sat around a fire away from society. I envisioned the things I was seeing and feeling would become an integral part of who I was, and the insight gained would bring me infinite satisfaction.

Mushrooms and peyote, among other things, have become an integral part of many cultures throughout history for a reason. The experience is gripping, and the heightened sense of awareness seems to wield truths of reality even after the drugs wear off. One's concept of what life "should be" grows closer to what life "really is." Unfortunately, the thrill of excess can create an affinity for the drug to a point of excess. It gets you high, and that always creates the possibility for addiction. Psychedelic addictions, unfortunately, can drive insanity. That night, I was trying to move past something in my life. I may very well have accomplished that, but what the future would hold was not what I was expecting.

A few weeks later I moved into my one-bedroom apartment in Morgantown. After the move-in, I envisioned a night alone around a fire at the beautiful Wonder Falls on the Lower Big Sandy Creek. I drove down to the Lower Big Sandy Creek with my backpack, and all my supplies and rations. It was Friday night, dark when I arrived, and I couldn't bring myself to do what I had been dreaming of for weeks. It was to be the next phase in my spiritual, psychedelic journey. I had dreamt of flames lighting the banks of Wonder Falls as I presided over the natural wonder alone, feeling the vibrations of the Great Spirit, and making my peace with that which so viciously disturbed me just a short time earlier in life. Epiphany, revelation, reverence. I thirsted for a place indigenous and endemic forever in these mountains. The journey I was embarking on would be stout. Mushrooms had a tendency to take me further than I wanted to go. I was afraid that I might bite off more than I could chew that night.

Afraid, I didn't even make it to Wonder Falls before I set up camp. I slept on a logging road without a fire. Daylight woke me in the morning. I packed up, and went back to my apartment. I was upset and disappointed with myself. My window of opportunity felt like it was closing. I felt as though if I were to do this, it had to be done now. Sunday afternoon I drove back to the place again. I walked in with my day-pack filled with a bag of mushrooms, an ounce of weed, a pipe, and a philosophy book written by Immanuel Kant, "The Critique of Pure Reason." It was early in the day when I made the mile and a half hike back to the waterfall. A great yellowish-brown sandstone bed stretched across the valley floor, bordered by rhododendron and hemlocks on either side. There were a few people nearby, drinking beer around a fire, and four-wheelers occasionally roaming about. I sat down on the river bed. I slipped my day-pack off my back and pulled out my reefer, my pipe, and "The Critique of Pure Reason." I smoked and began reading in the shade of the hemlocks, just listening to the trickle of water running over the ledge and dropping 18+ feet to the rocks below. A pair of high school kids caught my eye. They must have been swimming. The ledge offered vertical relief to the pool below. I only knew that bit of exhilaration from the cockpit of a kayak.

After I had gotten high and started making my way through my philosophy book, I pulled out the bag of mushrooms. Roughly three grams were encapsulated in the sandwich bag. I thought to myself "I can eat one cap, or the whole bag." I didn't have the ambition to follow my intentions drawn up on my last trip. The possibility of a gentle, gradual journey into the mind did not seem important. I didn't have the patience or commitment for such a journey. I didn't have the self-control, and the lack of such always leads to bad outcomes. I tilted the bag to my mouth and leaned my head back, devouring all of the fungus. The mushrooms were dry, and the granular texture that filled my mouth after munching down was gritty and parching. Some citrus fruit seemed to be a necessity. It cleansed the mouth and throat. All I had about me was a lemon, no oranges. I took a bite of lemon-wedge and choked down the sour citrus. I went back to the book for a while just listening to the water falling over the ledge into the pool below, and reading along. I pulled out the pipe and smoked for a while. After nearly an hour, I could feel the mushrooms taking effect. Back to the book it was. Kant was addressing the order of cosmic and terrestrial things in time, size, importance, and influence. He was critiquing reason. He placed order to the hierarchy of forces in our universe and talked about the paradigm of transcending experience directly into the teachings of reason and rationale. Reading comprehension is not at its peak under the influence of psychedelic mushrooms. Written thoughts appeared to me in bits and fragments, but subliminally I was taking it all in. The words I read, and the logic that organized those words adjusted my thoughts. Whether I wanted to experience it or not, pure reason would eventually take over.

After about an hour of reading about the order of influence of creation, visual hallucinations began to set in. It wasn't gradual. It hit me harder than a punch from Mike Tyson. First, there were the bombs falling from the sky. Recollection of a war waged manifested itself in the beginning of my hallucination. I had spent much of that summer with a military veteran. He was the only person in my community who could understand what I had gone through months prior. I had to fight for my life and the rest of the world felt unreal. I needed the connection. I'm not sure what prompted my look skyward, but I did look up. Black bombs with pink and green tails fell from the sky. It looked like something out of Super Mario Brothers. My heart rate increased, and I walked to the river bank taking shelter in the shade of a box elder.

The exhilaration of the bombs subsided, but the fungus left no time nor room for relaxation. I looked to the box elder, and saw glistening, voluptuous hearts dripping out of the leaves of the tree. It reminded me of Katie Jones. Feelings and desires of love laid before me. They were expressed in small portions, but plentiful in quantity. The moment was surreal. The color and dimension of the images before me popped and glistened in a way that captured my attention and connected with emotions. Then, tyranny filled my mind from instances of our past. The trainwreck that was Cheat Fest 2010 was drawn to the forefront of my cognition. Then I heard a sound, a sound like the biggest alarm clock in the world going off in my head, loud and fast. I was bewildered. The sensation was the same feeling that filled me as I watched Katie Jones sucking face with the short, fat, red-headed man at Cheat Fest just months prior. I looked to the sky, and saw two pairs of eyes without faces. They danced about, one with pink and the other with yellow outlines. They were elongated height-wise. They had no pupils, and mirror-lenses the shade of limpid pools of water. The eyes flashed and raced across the sky synchronized in time with the alarm clock in my head.

I was frightened. I pulled out my pipe, and smoked some more hoping to relax. After I smoked, I walked over to the ledge of Wonder Falls and just listened to the water hitting the pool of rocks and water below. I closed my eyes and relaxed for a moment. When I opened my eyes once again, I could see my consciousness looming over the 20'x40'X70' gulch below me. There was an outline of a three-dimensional skull filling the pool that the falls dropped into. The skull was electric light of green and white camouflage with specks of red. I thought I had left my body, and my swim seven months prior had captured my soul in that pool for all eternity. I marveled at the hallucination for a moment then turned to the shore. Noise began to fill my head. I looked out onto the valley walls and saw a huge ball of wet paint racing through the woods. It was taller than the trees and dripping with vibrant color. It looked like a ball with slices of every chromatic color of the spectrum, 80 feet in diameter. The full spectrum came to me in symbolism. All that is, was, and could possibly be was one unified entity. Though vivid, it was not definitive, but rather infinite. It raced across the forest from horizon to horizon, towards and away from me, back and forth with constant, intense, motion. I was certain it would run me over and I would drown in the spectrum of wet paint. To no relief, a half dozen four-wheelers and side-by-sides showed up out of nowhere. I thought they were out to get me. I was shitting my pants. I walked over to the men drinking beer around the fire to the side of the falls and asked for a dip of snuff. One of the men had Copenhagen Long Cut. I pinched the tobacco and placed it between my cheek and gum. After a few moments I gathered myself and left Wonder Falls. The walk out felt pagan and primal as my feet trudged along the dry logging road back to my car. I had slipped into the spirit world and I was avoiding serpents. Under the hot August sun, my feet burned in my boots as I walked the dry cracked road of dirt. I sat down to gather myself and took my boots off hoping I would return to reality soon. After leaving Wonder Falls I felt displaced. While there, among the crowd, I felt like a target. I wasn't sure how to find my place in life. Eating mushrooms wasn't the answer.

I could not make sense of what happened, but it was imbedded within me. Nothing new and Earth-shattering was revealed, or at least not in a manner that I could understand. My past engulfed the present, and I did not know how to move forward. It was all so impressive. All that I saw would stick with me for months, maybe years to come, maybe even the rest of my life. I made my way back to my apartment in Morgantown, and found a bottle of cranberry wine in my refrigerator. I drank the whole bottle trying to calm down from all that I had witnessed, and when the drink was gone I began smoking again. It did no good. I hoped the bud would relax me, and I could ease my way out of the trip. Instead it just sustained my hallucinations. Before the sun went down I remember standing in front of the mirror, and thinking "I don't know if I can do it. I don't know if I can complete a semester." That was one day before classes started.

Chapter 2: Sex

It was a Friday, the end of the third week of the
fall semester in Morgantown. That day I saw two nursing
students that I used to kayak with. After some smooth
talking, one of them invited me along for a night out in an
attempt to humor the other. I needed laid. I was a 22 year-
old college student and still a virgin. Hormones were
running wild within as I felt like a horny failure. I went to
the bar with the girls and tried to romance one of them all
night. She was not promiscuous or a heavy drinker so I had
my work cut out for me. She was hot though. Beautiful
face and hair, round bottom, and chesty. Her smile though,
her smile was impenetrable. It was innocent but her eyes
sparkled when she smiled at me, and every time she did my
heart would melt. It was hard to move past her beauty and
innocence. Her voice was something sexy and teased me
further towards something that was probably never going to
happen, premarital sex. Food and beer was had. No
marijuana was smoked that day, but I was far from sane
and sober. The work of the psychedelic mushrooms were
still shifting shapes in my mind and the world around me.
The platonic friend got a laugh as I tried to romance the girl
I had the hots for. I wasn't getting far and did little more

than give longingly gazes and stand in place to be gazed upon, myself. I smiled and made eye contact. We didn't talk much, and I made almost no physical contact. Nothing happened aside from me buying her a few beers. As we left the bar as a group, we said good-bye and I made my way back to the ghetto. I was fumbling with my keys, trying to open the door to my apartment, when the girl next-door approached me.

"Do you want a beer?" She asked. How could I say no? "Come on up," she invited me. She was in her early thirties, single with two kids, an attractive woman with red hair and glasses. We were introduced sometime prior in a weekend afternoon of beerpong. I remember looking at her that first day and getting aroused. She was a curvy redhead and talked with a sultry voice. When we were around each other I could tell she was into me, and it really turned me on. We smoked a cigarette on the balcony then walked in to her apartment. We were moving closer towards each other on some level as we talked and passed a bottle of rum back and forth. I was getting excited, but I felt relaxed. Everything was flowing and felt like it had continuity. We were on the same level, nothing to indicative of sex but both of us figured that was where things were going. I dropped some lines and was turning her on, and I was closing in on my big break. She excused herself to her bedroom and came out wearing a sexy little nightgown. I wasted no time. We started making out. I welcomed her return with a few long, succulent kisses then she asked if she could go down on me. Hands roamed, and lips caressed bodies. I stood over her and brushed her hair away from her face. Before I knew it, I found myself inside of her. Warm and wet, soft and hard, for the first time in my life. The thrill of sex was rushing through my veins. Our bodies moved, and every rhythmic movement brought us closer to harmony. We started slowly, then gradually accelerated until we were a flawed yet perfect "one". We were rushing with sensual stimulation, but she suppressed my kisses a little and that left me detached. With tongue blocking tongue, I couldn't fall deeply into the moment. It was grand and dysfunctional, but the moment was a climax. It was sensual and perverse, quick and dirty. Skin was a different high than the transcendental rise from psychedelic drugs. There was supposed to be a connection there, but the whole thing felt unwarranted. There was no love, just physical attraction in the here and now. After five or ten minutes it was over. I put my pants on and stepped outside to have a smoke with no shirt. She made devilish remarks about how hot I was, and our tandem party moved back to my apartment. We went to the floor, but I wasn't turned on enough to go for round two. She laid on her back nude and I kissed her body, but didn't plunge in to intercourse a second time. Cuddled, she asked to stay the night, but I turned her away. I made no connections with the soul and spirit of this woman, just hot dirty sex. What I imagined my first time to be was something far greater, something Earth-shattering. I was a little disappointed. After she left I felt like I failed her. I couldn't comfort the woman after intimacy. I spent the rest of the night alone. I wasn't very happy with myself. I gave her some bullshit story of how I needed to return to Johnstown early in the morning.

The night passed and I didn't sleep a wink. I just packed my things into my car through the night and smoked a few bowls. In early morning, just as the sky lightened to shades of grey, I turned the key in my ignition, and left Morgantown. The whole ride I home I became upset, even bitter about what had transpired the night before. I had felt robbed. I couldn't be satisfied with the dirty pleasure I felt. Maybe I had gone too far into my spirituality and theology with the mushrooms, and too far into morality and intellect with the LSD to fully enjoy the indulgence the night before. My head was a mess, constant negative thoughts. I just needed some time and space to gather myself. I dropped a few things off at home, and headed for the mountains. I knew of a range far out of the way, a ridgeline above where my father took me fishing when I became sure-footed enough to negotiate the craggy banks of Clear Shade Creek.

I arrived at the pull-off early Saturday afternoon, and grabbed my pack out of the back of my car. I had my sleeping bag, a tarp, cord, water, a saw, and the meagre remains of the ounce of marijuana I accrued a few weeks prior. I walked along a trail paralleling the creek for about two miles then began ascending the hillside until I reached the plateau along the eastern continental divide. I was at the top of Babcock Ridge. Anxiety, and resentment dissolved in the clean, mountain air. Glens of cherry and maple opened up to fields strewn with cherry and maple saplings. Small ferns and dried forbes littered the understory. The sky was still bright, but the sun was getting low in the sky. I tied up my tarp into a bivouac, cut enough firewood to get me through the night. With wood cut, and kindling gathered, I began tending to the flame. First was a bundle of forbes and grasses to catch a spark, then bigger and bigger wood was added slowly. I didn't rush. I took the time to breathe life into the fire, and let the flames grow and consume the wood. It was dark by the time the heartiest logs were added, chummers.

I sat back and smoked a few bowls, and watched the stars. I pondered the spirits that inhabited the legendary graveyard, Crumb Cemetary, that laid off in the woods a few miles downrange. Then I thought about new life that was taking its first steps on this beautiful planet. I watched the stars twinkle through smoke filled eyes, then glanced back at my own smoke and flames. The thought of a unified spirit filled my mind; unity in the wood, the smoke, the heat, the light, my soul, and the souls that left their mark on my life. I thought about the woman from the night before and what she meant to me. I thought about those who had given me opportunities and spent time with me in the wilderness. I felt love, true love.

Everything felt in place, and I didn't even consider the fact that I would have to leave my little piece of heaven behind come tomorrow. As the night drew on, and I grew bored with my hallucinations, I wanted to play a little game. Throughout that summer I felt as though I could direct my attention to the exact location of anywhere in the world, that is anywhere I had some connection to. Gauley Fest was next weekend, and I had a transcendental moment at Pillow Rock on the Upper Gauley the year prior. I would go as far as calling it spiritual and Earth-shattering. I directed my attention to where I felt Pillow Rock Rumbling far beyond the horizon, and I pulled out my compass. I jotted down the azimuth in the direction I suspected the great rapid to be in, and went to sleep. When I rose the next day, I broke down camp, packed my things and hiked the two miles back to my car, and left Babcock Ridge behind. I returned to Morgantown later that Sunday. I was a changed person. I felt small, so small that I had no purpose in life. Yet, I felt powerful. I felt as though I tapped into something mystical, and that power was at my expense. When I settled into my apartment that day, I pulled out my atlas, 217^0 from Babcock Ridge to Summersville Dam. My guess for Pillow Rock was right on.

Chapter 3: Gauley Acid

The third weekend of September finally arrived. It was that sacred weekend when the whitewater community from around the world converged on Summersville, West Virginia for the biggest whitewater festival on Earth, Gauley Fest. When the Friday arrived to leave Morgantown and head south down I-79, I was all balls. I had my orange Pyranha creek boat strapped to the roof of my Subaru Outback, and a backpack filled with just enough LSD and marijuana to get me through the weekend. After everything that had transpired that year, particularly the events regarding Katie Jones, I had a death wish, and I could think of no better place to spend my final day than on the Upper Gauley.

As I was leaving Morgantown, the sun was hot in the clear blue sky. It was sometime around 3 pm when I found myself in traffic waiting to get on the highway. Sitting idle on a street backed up by a stop sign, I looked in my rear-view mirror and saw a coal truck behind me. As I looked at its chrome bumper vibrating in the sunlight, the thought of what that truck at my posterior saw crossed my mind. "Doft-stylus" emanated through my brain. The words were peculiar, but few things bound by the realm of sanity evaded my thoughts those days. Overtones of Pittsburgese mixed with phonetics of sailors and seamen from ages past ran through my mind. That's where I tended to identify myself at that point in my life. I considered myself daft, nay, doft. And that orange skewer formed of molded plastic attached to my roof was my stylus. I inched my way towards the stop-sign and the highway. When I finally hit the four-lane, I accelerated to about 70 miles per hour and flowed with the traffic. I occasionally passed other vehicles with boats on their roof, and we would acknowledge each other with a smile and a peace sign.

It was around dark when I arrived at the campground. I don't recall much after the trip down. There wasn't an excess of smoke and booze. My intentions were set on the river. I was in deep focus from the moment I loaded the Subaru until I was at the river. Saturday morning came with stoic excitement. I knew what was afoot. I rallied with two paddlers from WVU, and a paddler from Johnstown. My pal from Johnstown ran his first descent of the Upper the year prior. The two paddlers from WVU never ran it before, and it took a little convincing to get them to put-on with us. We managed to get two cars to the put-in by mid-morning. When I began getting dressed for the river, I could not find my river shorts. I remembered where they were; in my apartment in Morgantown. I had a pair of neoprene pants in my bag for winter paddling, but that was all I had to cover the lower portion of my body. Fortunately they weren't too telling of my crotch. I slid my neoprene, short-sleeved shirt on, and dressed in all black neoprene I imagined my appearance to be Grasshopper, the student. We unloaded boats, and I packed a small jar with two squares of little, white paper inside into my dry box. With the boats off, one of my pals and his girlfriend ran shuttle. That gave me time to make repairs to my boat. Four months prior, I ran Paint Creek of the Stonycreek watershed at a bare-bones level. All the shallow slides put a crack in my boat about 7 inches long where the side of the boat met the bottom. I sat in the parking area for the Upper Gauley in my black neoprene Grasshopper suite with a stick of p-tex in one hand, and a butane lighter in the other.

For those of you not familiar with p-tex, it is a polymer used for repairing skis and snowboards with deep scratches in the base. It was the best idea I had to fix the crack in my boat for a single day's use. I melted the p-tex and patched the crack, and by that time my pal returned from running shuttle. The four of us jumped on the truck-and-wagon to take us from the upper parking area, a long grassy right-of-way dissected by a l road on top of a hill, down to the river side. We got close to the river, and unloaded. We grabbed our boats and walked the trail down to the riverside. The put-in for the Upper Gauley is at the base of Summersville dam, and the only good flows from the dry season come from the dam-release at a rate of 2,000 cubic feet per second. The release water was about 350 yards upstream of us roaring. I set my boat on the river's edge, and pulled out my dry-box. I unscrewed the lid of my little jar, and slipped a piece of little white paper under my tongue. There was one left, and I asked one of my pals if he too would like a hit of LSD before putting-on to the most prestigious river in the eastern U.S. He declined. We climbed in our boats, and slid skirts over cockpits, then launched.

We came up on Initiation in a hurry. I was in the zone. I knew what I was doing was high risk, but I was certain the rewards would be beyond anything I could imagine… if only I knew. We crashed through the first class IV rapid, Initiation, and it was on! My repair work seemed to be keeping the water out of my boat, as we made our way through a few class III and IV rapid. I became jittery with anticipation and inner tension as the LSD began to set in. I don't know what made me more nervous, the drug or the river. By the time we made it to the first class

V rapid, the LSD had begun to set in with noticeable effect. Insignificant roared just below the horizon. I remembered the line from the last year: Come in right of center and move left as fast as you can, miss the enormous hole in the middle of the river and the undercut rocks on the right. I led the way. I looked at the bottom of the rapid and traced a line back to the top, planning every move along the way. The whitewater formed a crystal, white track along the line I was planning to crash. I dropped over the horizon with my boat angled in the direction I wanted to move. I timed my paddle strokes with the current. I hit the big peaks and stayed out of the deep, low swales. I found harmony in the most raucous of water and rose and fell with every successive wave, gaining amplitude as the wavetrain ran downstream. My two pals from WVU weren't far behind when I eddied out at the bottom of the rapid, but my pal from Johnstown was nowhere to be seen. As my worry escalated I saw his little, red play-boat cruise past the big hole in the middle of the rapid, and bob down the runout. We fraternized, the four of us, when we all sat at the bottom of Insig', then paddled on.

The sun reflected and refracted from the white spray coming off the river, sparkling like a technicolor beacon guiding me as we cruised down the next 3 miles of class III and IV whitewater. It wasn't long before we came to a portion of the river where all the water choked down to the left side of the river and crashed against Pillow Rock with its exploding white spray. We got out on the right and took a look. I stood at the shore of the river with my closest friend from WVU with an arm extended and my voice as loud as I could muster to be heard over the roaring river. "Come in left of the peaks. By the third wave you want to be on the right side of the wavetrain moving right as hard as you can go. That's all there is to it." He was working up the gumption to run the most intimidating rapid on the river when I hopped in my boat and fired up the line. I took my own advice and came in left of the peaks of the wavetrain with some right angle, moving right. The rushing water was rolling up and down with 5 foot waves. It was fast and steep. By the third wave I was well far enough over to miss the huge exploding spray coming from pillow rock. Just before the pillow I found myself facing upstream surfing a six foot wave that was rushing past at 2,000 cubic feet of water per second. It was big and awesome. The acid was reeling in my brain at about that time. I couldn't believe the energy that was flowing under my boat and pulsing through my veins. I wasn't getting visual hallucinations, but every sense was crisp and clear and vivid. The light was bright, and the sound was loud, but clear. I could feel the rock and the enormous pillow of water, 14' x 8' x 8', behind me. It was like a monster prowling, but I danced with the river. The pillow pushed me forward and I harmonized with the raucous water, escaping its grasp. Eventually I saw another paddler bearing down the second class V of the day, so I twisted just a bit, turning my boat to river-right, surf-left, and ferried into the eddy just right of the main flow. I watched my three pals run their lines with little drama, and we worked our way downstream just a hair. We were nearly 4 miles in to the 12 miles of river, and my right leg was falling numb. I wasn't the only one with sore hips and legs. The rest of the crew decide to join me on Pillow Rock. We paddled just downstream, behind the enormous boulder. We dragged our boats ashore and climbed up onto the boulder. There was a crowd of people watching paddlers run their lines down Pillow. The four of us stood on the rock amongst the crowd for a moment then I snuck off to the woods to smoke. When I returned the rest of my crew was nowhere to be found. I thought they left me. I wasn't about to leave until I knew for sure, so I took in all the sights and sounds. Most of the people on Pillow Rock were through middle aged men and women. There was also one boy maybe 12 years old standing on Pillow Rock, watching paddlers go by.

After my smoke the river really came alive. The sun brightened. The rock trembled beneath my feet. The spirit from within me, and the spirit outside from the sun and the river that fed life into a small plant growing on that boulder. I moved in step around it, synchronizing my heartbeat and footsteps with the trembling from the river. The light broke, and the plant seemed to dance. The leaves, and shoot, and blossom twisted in color with cool, vivid hues. I stepped about the rock for a while, watching paddlers jump 12 feet into the river below, below the meat of the rapid, but still in swift water including 12 year old boy. I thought about it, but memories of Wonder Falls lingered in my mind. This wouldn't kill me, but it might send me into fear for the rest of the day. What felt like 45 minutes went by and I concluded my pals left without me. I scampered back down to my boat and embarked on the final 8 miles without my pals.

A long line of class IV rapids were to follow, and the acid was in full effect. 2 miles later was the next class V rapid, Lost Paddle. I was all alone, and I had no one to rely on for advice on a line or a rescue. I remembered nothing from Lost Paddle the year before. Fortunately everything was clear. I was approaching nirvana. I saw my lines before me as if they were painted on the water with sunlight. The approach was in the center of the river, then the whole flow moves right, towards some undercuts, and pillows up into a huge curling wave that bends back to the left. I dropped the horizon, and the acid started shifting gears. I felt the black of my suit and the orange of my boat. I felt like a Hessian with a paddle in hand, maybe just German to the core. The rhythm of the river was roaring, and I was tripping. I felt time, I felt harmony. I wanted to dance, and fortunately I had the best partner God ever created, class V whitewater. I floated right with some left angle and became dangerously close to crowding out another kayaker as I hit the Hawaii Five-O wave a little sideways. When I hit the runout, I was bumpin! I was in the heart of the river, all alone, with a headful of acid. It was bas-ass. I wanted to dance, and dance I did.

About a mile and a half later I came to Iron Ring, the fourth class V rapid. One small frowny-face-hydraulic sits above the rapid on river-right. A second frowny-face-hydraulic sits just below that, nearly twice as large, extending from left to center. This rapid is known to have claimed lives consistently throughout history. I sat in the eddy above the rapid, alone, just cooling in the moment. The eddy was shady, and it was early afternoon on a beautiful West Virginia weekend. It was the weekend that many like myself consider the last weekend of summer. As I sat in the eddy, and looked over the options, two lines stuck out. I could move through some boulders close to the middle of the river, or skirt both holes and hit 9 foot standing wave just between them. A couple, two kayakers in playboats, came in as I sat there.

"What do you think the line is?" I asked.

"Skip between the boulders," he replied.

I thought about what he said, and what was visible before me. I nodded at his advice but chose my own line. I peeled out. I skirted the hole on the right then the one on the left and stitched a line headlong into the 9 foot standing wave. I never made it to the top. Instead I pierced right through the water as it was still rising towards the heavens. I subbed-out completely and felt the embrace of Creation while I was under water. I couldn't breathe and was surrounded by fluid. Still I was in my boat. The life-blood of Creation had engulfed me, and I was waiting to be spat out the backside of the wave. I was below the surface but felt so safe, and so unified with the Great Spirit. When I popped out of the wave upright on the downstream side, I could only think of one word; an old Indian word for people, Nimipu.

I was getting over my concerns about paddling alone at this point. Only one class V rapid remained,

Sweet's Falls. Just before Sweet's, the river bends gently to the left with a beautiful cliff river-right shooting up to the sky. There were some boulders just left of the main flow before the drops over the horizon. Sweet's falls is a 12 foot long, nearly vertical tongue, that plunges deep, and the bottom is bordered by toilet bowls on both sides, and a big aerated curler punctuates the tongue as rises back up to meet placid water A familiar face drifted through the canyon along my side, it was Bob Spangler. His long black hair and sun-kissed skin delivered some comfort in familiarity. I asked him what the line was when I realized where we were. I needed no explanation. I was just nervous. Hey-diddle-diddle, right down the middle. Bob eddied out behind the boulders on river-left and I decided to run the drop right away. I saw two mini curlers at the top, bending right, and I approached it from the right with some left angle. I hit the tongue and accelerated downwards, slowly rotating my boat to the right as I descended. I hit the bottom in a hurry then came up over the curling waves that rise from the bottom of the waterfall. Just as I came up, my bow broke through the punctuating curling reactionary, and before it could rock me back, I leaned into it. I grabbed a paddle full of whitewater, bracing myself and running the thing cleanly. I was elated. Sweet's Falls was one of two place where I went upside-down the year prior. This year I championed it. My drop was met with celebration from all the paddlers looking on from the shore.

"Ole`, ole` ole` ole`, ooole` ole`!" erupted when I was in the pool below.

Words can't describe the feeling I had that day, that place, that moment. When I arrived at the take-out, I was alone. That I knew. I figured either I would be greeted by my pals when I walked up to the parking area, or they weren't off the river yet. They weren't there, and neither was my car which was supposedly left there in the shuttle. A problem, yes. A big problem, no. The whitewater community is a resilient bunch. One of our best skills is composing logistics on the fly. I was a little upset that they hadn't waited for me to get off the river before the three of them took my car back to camp… if that's what happened.

Anyway, I searched the lot for a vehicle that had room on the roof or in the bed for one more boat. There was a man in dry clothes standing beside his Toyota Tacoma with room in the bed for one more boat.

"Hey! Are you heading back to the campground?" I asked.

"Yeah."

"Got room for one more?"

He said yes a second time. I was elated. The day hadn't gone exactly as planned, but it turned out better than expected. I didn't have any dry clothes packed in my boat, and I felt a bit chilly in the shady lot. We loaded up my boat and I hopped in the back seat of the truck. The takeout road for the Upper Gauley is about five miles of dirt road that twists and turns as it rolls up, over, and down the hills of West Virginia. Sunlight peeked through the shade of the trees, and shined bright on the meadows along the road. I began to warm up and dry off just a bit in the truck. The temperature change sent the LSD shifting gears. The trip that mellowed out by the end of the river had come on strong in a new wave with the new comfort I was feeling. Every flower that we passed seemed to turn its blossomy head towards me and spin as we went by. Three lines, one red, one green, and one black descended from the sky in neon color connecting me, the flowers, and the campground all together. The ride back to camp was about 45 minutes long. When I arrived at the campground, I was surprised to find that my pals hadn't returned from the river yet. That got me thinking, "Maybe I was ahead of them. Maybe my car was in a different lot." If they were waiting for me at the take-out, I couldn't imagine what worries were going through their minds. I was a little worried, myself. I had no proof of their circumstance though, so I went about my business. I finished drying off, changed, and brushed my hair. I had dark, seafoam green work slacks, and a button up fishing shirt with a collar, and white, blue, and green cross-hatched stripes. I had the hipster vibe going that evening, and I was lookin' sharp! Food and beer was in order after such a day. I ate and drank, and got to smoking. Within an hour or two, my pals returned with my car.

"What happened!" I asked.

"You left us behind at Pillow." They replied.

We laughed knowing that not much of that mattered now. The important part was that everyone was safe and sound back at camp, ready for a night of revelry.

The jar I kept the LSD in had a rusty lid. I didn't think that would matter at all. It turns out I was wrong. The rusty scent and taste worked its way into my brain and as I came down off the trip that night, my entire body felt jangly and metallic. I felt like a tuning fork. The day turned to night and waves of acid came and went. Gauley Fest is rather classy for a whitewater festival. It's not exactly a drug seen, although plenty of herb is smoked, and a few individuals bring in the occasional ration of hallucinogens. Once darkness fell, it felt like a carnival. In a sense it was. All the vendors reminded me of the County Fair. I hallucinated the phrase "For all your deer!!!" as it emanated through my head. I didn't know what the wager was over, or who I was wagering against, but I was willing to bet 'all my deer'. Maybe it was on the grounds that Katie Jones did or did not have the cutest ass known to the whitewater community. Who knows. I skipped and frolicked about the festival in the same fashion I spent the day on the river, flying solo. The band was playing bluegrass and I crossed paths with a female river guide I worked with in Ohiopyle. We danced, and as I looked in her eyes I only felt a longing to see Katie one more time. In the back of my mind, I expected to see curly-Jones in the crowd just as I had the year before. I wanted to see her, and it felt like we had some unfinished business after Cheat Fest. The carnival rolled on for a few hours with bluegrass in the air, and 'for all your deer!' in my head. The party came to an end, and the after party began. Depending on who shows up to the festival, sometimes that means boxing matches. This year the South Carolina boys showed up, and brought the gloves along.

"Who's gonna fight Jesse!" the oldest man in the camp next to us exclaimed.

Jesse stood about 5'11'' and 240 pounds. My dimensions on that day were roughly 6'1" 155lbs, but I spent about a month training at a fight club in Morgantown earlier that year. My head was big. The trainer complimented me every week on my boxing. My wrestling ability in the club was unmatched, and I figured I had more skill than Jesse had size.

Jesse screamed at me while we strapped the gloves on trying to intimidate me. I just sauntered from side to side, quietly, while I went into my mind and felt every nerve, muscle, and ligament in my body. I thought about quick jabs and fast footwork. I thought about that moment spent subsurface at the Iron Ring earlier that day. We touched gloves and it was on. I came out of the hole firing. I landed a solid jab right off the whistle, and sent Jesse back on his heels. Two more rights, and a left, and he was about on the ground. I went to finish him off with one more right, but got sloppy in form. I exposed my face, and as I threw what should have been the final right hand, he ducked my jab, and came up with a hard fist of his own as my body got too far out in front of my feet. That punch broke my rhythm, and with it, my concentration. I held my arms up weakly in front of my face as Jesse proceeded to break my guard. The second punch sent me moving backwards, and I was standing every inch of six feet tall with my head tilted back when the third punch connected right under my nose. I hit the ground. I was hoping to win the bout before he could even land a single punch. I didn't anticipate the pain of battle. As I knelt on all four's, I came to a quick decision: Jesse won.

We drank beer together after the match since their crew was camped directly beside us. The metallic feeling in my body got stronger, and I snuck off to my tent and crashed for the night. The next morning hummed with talk of Sunday-paddling. I had my day on the Upper G, and was ready to go home. I felt like an outlaw. I felt like something did not sit well between me and the authorities. Possibly out of sheer anxiety, I feared the law was hunting me. As I bought a little bud to hold me over till I could get back to Morgantown, I felt like my image was being magnified and displayed just above the horizon. I tried to hide beneath the collar of my shirt so my face wouldn't project to the sky. With all provisions taken care of for the ride back, I walked over to get breakfast at the cafeteria at the edge of the campground. Along the way I saw a face I was familiar with from a kayaking movie I owned. It was Eric Jackson. We introduced ourselves, shook hands and shared a smile. That was just enough good humor to make me forget about my lost boxing match the night before.

Chapter 4: Archery Season

The Weekend after Gauley Fest was the first weekend of archery season in Pennsylvania. It was the first year I had ever hunted with a recurve. Earlier that year I traded in my compound bow for a traditional piece of archery equipment. I wanted a a new challenge. The first morning of the season was dull. The mountain I hunted was being logged, and there were no signs of deer, but my mind was off somewhere else. All the mental stress from weeks and months past left me envisioning a forest of supernatural energy. I believed I could communicate with any person anywhere on Earth. All I needed to direct my energy was my wicket, my bow.

The morning was spent still-hunting, slowly creeping through the hollow beneath the trees. I was receiving and sending energy in a wizardly fashion. By late morning I left the woods to get some food and meet up with other hunters at the bottom of the mountain. The air was warm and the skies were clear. I was catching sunlight as it refracted through whatever water droplets lined the swamps and meadows. Bright, vibrant yellows caught my eye, and my gullet hummed in deep, gravely delight. The other hunters came down from their stands. We ate and relaxed in the early autumn noon. As we sat around the picnic table and ate lunch, I envisioned our realm warping. Color harmonized with sound, and personalities portrayed supernatural, visible personas, not only with the people at camp, but the food, flora, and fauna. Time ticked in my mind, and seemed to bend at my will. The meter and frequencies of our voices seemed to warp the atmosphere, and I believed reality had dissolved into a realm.

I spent every weekend chasing whitetails with no success. A portion of the time was spent fixing my head to perceive nature as I thought it existed in its essence; something pure, and supernatural. My heady still-hunting was little more than a delusion. I was falling into time with the rhythm of the forest, but I was also hallucinating relationships between my spirit and the spirit of the wild. I thought I knew what laid beyond the horizon. I only drew back on one deer that fall, and it never presented a good shot. In high school I read bits of a book written by Fred Bear on the topic of still-hunting. He said sometimes you might need to run to get a good shot at a deer. To this day I'm not sure I know what he meant because at one point that fall, I sprinted through the woods after some doe. If I would have been capable of landing a solid 60 yard shot, I would have been able to prove those words true. I was hunting on a knob of mixed forest. Most of the timber was mature oak trees with hemlocks mixed in. I was traversing a flat on my way out of the forest at dusk when I came across the deer. I saw them raise their tails, and I heard leaves crunching as they ran off through the grape-vines. Now was my chance to put Fred Bear's words to the test. I took off running after the two doe through the young trees and grape vines. The deer didn't run far, but they heard me coming like and ice-wagon. I closed in as they stood still, but by the time they crossed my sight they were on the run again. I chased after them again with the same result. I think I'll retire that hunting technique.

Chapter 5: Fall Semester

Fall waned on. It was late October when I was headed back to Morgantown from Johnstown. The car was packed full of laundry and groceries. I exited the highway in the rainy night and came to a traffic light in the Westover section of town. The light was red. I stopped and the engine died. Most of the way across I-68 my thermostat was running hot, and I was concerned. I pulled over at one point and filled the radiator with water. I must have blown a hose in the cooling system because the temperature of the engine never dropped. It over heated and cracked the engine block. The car lasted just long enough for me to get back to Morgantown. A vehicle pulled up behind me at the traffic light with my engine dead. The driver got out and we pushed the car into the parking lot of a service station that was located at the corner of that intersection. I asked the driver for a lift back to my apartment with a few bags of groceries in hand. He gave me a ride, and once I dropped my things at my apartment I set out for Westover to carry back the rest of what I could that night. It was a depressing moment and I had a lot of time to think about things. It seemed fitting. I was still wallowing in the dither Katie Jones had sent me into months earlier. I began to put distance between me and my friends. When I thought about my family I just got angry. They wanted the best for me, but I believed the man they conditioned me to become was a failure. The walk from Westover back to my apartment was dark and cold and wet. The rain and the night were my only friends, and uncomfortable friends they were. That night they did a good job of hiding the tears that often fell. Rage and sadness were in constant flux with each other, and as I searched for a suspect, I only found myself. I spent many a night sitting at the kitchen table with a knife laid out in front of me, just thinking, "Is tonight the night I end it?" All that kept me from shoving that steel into my skull was the thought of how bad it would be for those who love me, how selfish and cowardly suicide really is.

I finally made it back to my apartment with a laundry bag of clean clothes. I cooked some rice, ate, and smoked a bowl. I sat in my armchair, and thought about hunting, and the mountain, and the deer-woods. That was my fantasy. That was the only place I felt at home, but that was remote from my current environment and current state of mind.

Monday started with a call to AAA to have my car towed back to Johnstown. The engine needed repaired.

The air was cool in Morgantown that week as October came to an end. I had one hit of LSD left in my stash. I ate it one afternoon, and went grocery shopping as I waited for it set in. I was making the two mile walk back from the grocery store back to my apartment along the Monongahela River when my mind began to shift. Patterns in the treeline formed and turned colors. Pink and black and yellow camouflage filled my eyes and a tune filled my ears on bass. After returning to my apartment I felt restless. I walked the town for a while. I looked to the south where my best friend and the Gauley River sat in the hills of southern West Virginia. And as I stood on a bridge looking down on the Monongahela River, I knew this would be the last time I would ever do LSD. The thrill and excitement of the drug sat second class to those sensations and hallucinations I perceived that day on the Upper Gauley River with a head full of acid. That trip would eternally overshadow any and all others. It was a depressing revelation, but a revelation none the less. I made my way back to my apartment in the night, and when I returned I was greeted by the powerplant humming loudly nearby. It was enough to make my eyes bulge with wry irritation. I couldn't relax. The powerplant had been an object of irritation since the day I moved in, something I overlooked when scouting for apartments. The pitch wasn't the problem. It was the volume constantly emanating from generator. The trucks pulling in to, and out of the plant was no pleasure. Diesel engines and air brakes blew at all hours. When I was at the place, I never had a moment to relax and ignore the damn thing. It drove me crazy.

As time passed I fell deeper and deeper into depression. The hallucinations from trips and traumas past echoed through my senses. It wasn't just the drugs. Every time I had a brush with death, and all the heartbreak from Katie Jones skewed my perception of reality. When I sat in my armchair I could see spires of color rise and fall out of the carpet. Faces showed primal features that fed my concept of a person's character. I could see lines along the lips and eyes that may, or may not have existed, but seemed to reveal opinions and outlooks upon life. I looked upon the faces of ramblers and scholars, vagrants and professionals, and everything in between. Few happy people sported expressions that matched what I felt inside. The more people I faced, the lonelier I felt. Eventually the supernatural was what I felt the greatest connection with. The physics, or maybe better yet, the metaphyics of the world around me held my attention. The noise from the powerplant just outside my apartment sparked my contemplation of ultrasonic vibrations. I spent a lot of time thinking about how those vibrations could alter the fabric of reality. I wondered if those vibrations should have a spiritual source, what power could they have over health. And, my computer, phone, and flash drive seemed to constantly fail me. I pointed at the supernatural. I got in my car and the tape-deck made strange sounds. The external speaker in my iPod really threw me for a loop. I thought Jimi Hendrix was speaking to me from the otherside when I unplugged the earbuds from the device. Technology made little sense to me up to this point in my life, and my perception of it at this time was deceiving me even further.

Life was a regular trainwreck. As one day turned into the next, they successively and perpetually became worse and worse. Mind, body, and spirit were completely out of balance, and I had little connection with the truths and constants of reality. One peculiar morning, I woke up and I sat up in bed. I felt no ambition. It was worse than laziness. I felt zero strength. It was as though I completely atrophied. I pushed myself onto my feet. I felt as physically drained as the day I laid breaths from death as a result of poorly prescribed care in a drug rehabilitation facility. My mind didn't feel as vacant as that day when a nurse stood over me and yelled "code blue" into her radio, but I felt weak. I dragged myself into the shower. The hot water made me feel even weaker, and more tired. I turned off the water and dried off, trying to muster some energy. I couldn't. I felt exhausted. I was scared. I had been running on fumes for a long time, and it finally caught up with me. Physically and mentally, I pushed myself to the limit. I finally had nothing left in the tank. I was afraid to spend much time on my feet for fear of fainting. This was a scary day. My most physically demanding days didn't leave me as tired as I felt on that cold November morning. I can't remember if I made it to my 8 o'clock class, but eventually I regained strength by afternoon. The concept of the supernatural working to destroy my health played on my mind.

As the rest of the semester unraveled, my perception continued to fail me. My concept of the world around me was a matrix woven around fallacies, fallacies that I would argue were true, and possibly could have convinced a few people of, but nothing made sense. I was heading down, but I was about to get out of Morgantown for the next to my last semester.

December came along with final's week. I studied my ass off trying to finish strong. The toughest class I had was a geography class called Remote Sensing. It was based around the science of satellite imagery and aerial photography. Lens-filters seemed to shade my eyes during class, and while studying. I believed if I could see the world as these cameras did, I would have a leg up on the rest of the class. Vision and optics were crisp and clear and more incorrect than 70 or 80% of the rest of my reality. It wasn't all in vain. I got a B+ on my term paper and presentation, and all I had to do make a solid showing on the final exam. I studied for that final engulfed with diligence, and It was the last test I had to take. Thursday afternoon I showed up to the classroom at 3pm. The door was locked, the lights were off, and the room was empty. Oh shit! I read the schedule wrong, and I missed the biggest exam of the semester. I thought my academic career was shot. I was frantic. I was beyond crying in misery. I was giving running away serious consideration. I thought I should just clean out my bank account, pack my bag, grab my bass, and board a train for Seattle. Running away looked more attractive than facing the music. Something inside of me held on to responsibility and a positive direction. I made my way to the geography department's computer aided mapping lab, and ran into my lab instructor. She said the professor was still around, and I should send him an email explaining my situation. Desperately, I did. It was the best chance I had. My prayers were answered when my professor told me to meet him in his office in half an hour. I took the test by myself.

I performed horribly, but I didn't score a zero. It was good enough to get a D+ for the semester.

Chapter 6: Fasting

With one more disaster narrowly avoided, I returned to Johnstown for a four week break between semesters. Rifle season for whitetail deer already ended, but I had a different fervor of buck fever. Late archery would soon come into season. Until then I was bound and determined to do some winter camping by myself. It was the shortest day of the year, the winter solstice. That little creek that gouged a scar into Babcock Ridge was in my mind. The ridge top was a bit too raw for me to spend longest night of the year. Nevertheless, I hiked back the ravine of Clear Shade Creek, two miles deep, on the afternoon of December 21st and began sawing dead timber. It was brisk in the daylight, somewhere in the neighborhood of 20 degrees Fahrenheit, but the hike in warmed me up. I fell and sawed snags with only a T-shirt and a turtle-necked sweater. The sun was getting low in the sky when I had about six poles fell and sawn. The foot of snow on the ground made gathering kindle rough. There was little pitch and tinder that I could collect. I scraped up what I could and went to work on the flame. I gave it a half-assed attempt, ignorant of what the night held for me. I thought hot tea, oatmeal, my tent, and sleeping-bag would be enough for me to bear the cold of the night. I gave up on the fire after about 20 minutes and retired about a half hour before dark. I was far from sleeping and took no smoke with me. I was restless. I managed to fall asleep a few hours after the sun went down, then it began to get cold. I woke up in the middle of the night and cooked some oatmeal and brewed some tea on my jet boil. It wasn't enough. I couldn't warm up. I kept at it for a few hours then the tent and the bag couldn't keep me from the cold. It was somewhere below zero on the thermometer around the time I crawled out of the tent. I went back to work on the fire and sparked up a modest blaze. It delivered some warmth, but it was a lot of work to keep it going. I had no small-to-medium sized firewood to make a powerful transition from spark to blaze. It was about 3:30 in the morning when I couldn't take it anymore. The cold was biting at my bones, and all I could think of was Katie Jones. Things were bitter. I tore down my tent and stuffed it into my pack along with my sleeping bag hastily and began the hike out. I decided to carry the steel bucksaw instead of lashing to my pack. The job I did stuffing my sleeping bag and tent into my pack wouldn't allow for it. My gloves were thin and about halfway back to the car, my hands throbbed with pain from carrying the frigid metal. By the time I made it to the car it was sometime after 4 AM and my hands felt as though they had been smashed with a hammer. I stomped and winced as they painfully regained feeling. I wondered if it was possible to get frostbite in such a manner. I sat in my car, and as I let the engine warm, my only thought was that I had failed at yet another thing in life. I couldn't conquer the winter on the mountain by myself. Poor planning sported a piss poor performance.

Days before the camping attempt I prepared the first cut of "River Class" for its first round of editing. When Christmas passed and late-archery began, I was ready to start editing my book. The holidays weren't festive. I was bitter from what happened in rehab the February prior, and somehow held my parents responsible. I spent Christmas detached, and it all ended in a big argument. I welcomed the first day I could return to the woods with a bow and arrow, and chase whitetails through the hills and hollows. And, I needed meat for the spring semester in Morgantown. The frigid, snow-covered hills offered comfort from all the trials that had worn me down in life. I just wanted to hunt, and enjoy all the simple pleasures hunting had to offer. I tried to tap the spiritual essence of the woods and the wildlife this time. I planned to fast from eating for the first three days of hunting season, and see what revelations Mother Nature would reveal to me. Information about Native American fasting rituals, and a day to myself without a meal left me intrigued and gave me the idea.

Hypoglycemia provides its own profound highs. I just didn't realize how profound they would be. The first day of late archery was very cold. The morning hunt began with hike up a long hillside in deep snow. I made it to the top, and I was in ecstasy. The world was white and quiet. I had a bag of marijuana and as I settled into the morning, I faced a decision: Should I or shouldn't I smoke? I packed a pipe, and took a few long drags. When I came up, a whirlwind kicked up in hollow below, and I saw four frozen marbles in the blowing snow and frosted forest. They were small and all differently colored. One red, one, yellow, one blue, and one green. I thought they were before me for me decide a fate. Maybe that's what it was. I chose the blue one, and took it as my own. I felt blessed by nature, and I was elated with the beginning of my road. I felt it was a message that, should I complete my fast for three days and three nights, I would kill my first deer with a recurve bow that hunting season. My feet were getting cold late in the morning and I returned home to warm up. That evening when I returned to the woods, I watched over a trail. I saw a red fox silently trot through the forest. The fox looked warm. Its rusty red fur and black ears were thick and plush. The wind swirled snowflakes into the air and the fox couldn't look more comfortable. Its little black paws pranced through the snow in complete silence and I was in awe of its beauty.

Late December 2010 was the first time I looked at "River Class" since I had written the manuscript. Editing started slow, then began flowing. I relived my life as I read along. The time alone in the frozen wilderness gave me inspiration for writing. The mind feeds on the free-form of nature. As I spent the next day on a hill a few miles away from home, I smoked and hunted feeling a deep connection with the forest. Ideas about the way to tell the stories of kayaking, work in the wilderness, and love gained and lost became clearer. I connected with the ebbs and flows of nature and I now knew what to say.

As I hunted, I felt like I was part of the wilderness, clothed in woolen camouflage. My right hand was cold from only wearing my shooting glove. I kept moving to keep my body warm. In late afternoon I spotted four doe on the hillside below me along a thicket. I moved in quietly on the soft snow. I was roughly 45 yards away from the closest deer. I stood at the edge of a pocket, empty of cover. I never thought of moving in ahead of them and only thought about a direct flank. They moved out without me ever being able to take a shot. As I made my way back to my car in the dark, my hand grew colder and colder. I pulled my keys from my pocket, and tried to turn the key in the lock. I had no strength in my hand. I used my left, awkwardly, and as I drove home I fell to fear instead of faith. I feared my body would shut down if I failed to feed it. Instead of having faith in my fast, I succumbed to my Earthly wants and needs.

The skillet smelled savory with butter as I thawed haddock and venison, and cut my onions. I fried the fish in the butter with onions and sage, then cleaned the skillet and seared some venison in Italian dressing. I was fat and happy. In my mind I was desperately in need of amino acids. I had been hallucinating small schools of fish all day, and all I could think of was "a-minnows". I successfully replenished my aminos. The sharp contrast between fasting and feasting set my bowels into shock as I was walking into the woods the next day. I was roaring from the end that you usually don't.

The hunting season lasted two weeks. I failed at my first attempt for fasting for three days. The deer-woods were no less interesting because of it. I roamed the winter hills with my pipe and bow, dawn to dusk, day after day, and every evening I returned home to edit "River Class." Life was ideal. All I was doing was hunting, writing, and smoking. Sparks of mystical psychedelic possibilities of a three day fast still illuminated my imagination after those first two days of the hunting season. The small mental and sensual incantations that I seized on that first attempt stuck with me even after the fast ended. The woods came alive, and I was part of that living, breathing ecosystem. As I walked slowly through the field and forest, along thickets and creeks, every cover type revealed its personality. Shape and color of vegetation was accented by its desires. The edge where vegetation types changed painted a mosaic where food and cover ebbed and flowed across the topography. Thick brush had a pesky humor about it, and the tall pines and the tall oaks towered over the land with stoic antiquity. The roughness of the trees, grass, and brush resonated their own unique audible tones, and the way they caught light and reflected the snow revealed secrets of each's character.

I moved the way the creatures of the forest naturally move, with rhythm and rest. Life revolved around the sun and the moon. I connected with the rhythm of the day, and moved in harmony with the lengths and meters that natural, primal metabolism follow. I felt like a great enigma. I believed that the forest was at my will, and I was seeing into the frequencies that soothed and relaxed the woody stems and grasses. The dormancy of plants in the winter didn't cross my mind as I quaked about hoping to get the plants to release their perfume from their pores. The sap of their circulatory system appeared to be under my persuasion. Everything seemed to be under my persuasion. I was beginning to speak the language of the Great Spirit. It was not all beauty, though. The winter was cold, and the pain those frigid temperatures brought were damning. Loud noises exploded in my mind at times, and when they would, pain would explode in my joints. I believed I was falling victim to voodoo or black magic by someone I may have crossed in the past. The pain I felt surge through my body and the voices in my mind left me angry with the world.

The second and final week of the season was waning, and I hadn't seen any deer since the second day. I hunted the same hills long and hard and was fruitless. I was desperate to get some shooting at a deer. Thursday night I made an agreement with myself to complete the three-day-fast before classes began at WVU the following week, no matter what the cost. Friday and Saturday came and passed. I spent both days hunting from dawn to dusk, and the evenings were spent getting things ready for the move back to Morgantown. I still saw no deer, but when Sunday came I refused to indulge in a meal.

In early afternoon I headed out of Johnstown. I wanted to spend my final hours of hypoglycemia somewhere special. I exited I-68 at Coopers Rock and headed for the Lower Big Sandy. When I got to the Rockville Bridge, I grabbed my pack and a few effects and headed for Wonder Falls. When I got to the snow covered flat overlooking the creek, there was an older man taking in the peace and inspiration I came to indulge in. His face was brazen from many years of sun. His skin was tight with a gentle smile on his face and a look of wisdom in his eye. I said hello, and he left shortly after I arrived. I laid down a tarp, took my boots off, and sat cross legged. I smoked and felt a deep connection with the waterfall. The incident was not psychedelic like the mushroom trip there months prior, but there was something mystical between my spirit and the Great Spirit. I couldn't quite put my finger on it, but maybe it's better that way. Mystery leaves room for amazement in the beauty of the world around us. The sun was getting low in the sky, and I packed everything up and began walking out. As I did, I felt as though I stretched in height to somewhere near 11 feet. The treetops seemed to bow down before me and I walked at eye-level with the ridge-line. At will, my height receded and I shrunk to a few inches tall. I believed I finally achieved the power to shape-shift. With the power of shape-shifting and speaking to the spirit of the wild, I also developed fears, delusions. I thought everything that was not natural was capable of disease, cancer. I began to limbo. I truly thought that if I shape-shifted and directed my energy just so, I would live forever and the artificial world around me would shrivel and die. I became easily irritated by everyone who didn't follow the supernatural understanding of our relationship between the individual and the world around us.

Chapter 7: Insanity

After that first meal in Morgantown, I smoked a pipe of marijuana. The river roared in my veins and the light and sound of raucous, greenish-blue water rumbled at my breast. I felt the strength of the waterfall in my shoulders, and down through my arms, into my hands. I only knew one other man who had lived through such a swim as I had at Wonder Falls, and I was curious; what of him? Every time we crossed paths on the river, at the bar, or at a party, I waited for the particular wavelength, the one my mind feasted upon and my body indulged its hallucinations. When that frequency infected the airwaves, I felt as though he and I overtook the room. I felt as though we were unmatched, intellectually and physically. The walls rumbled about us, and tyrants seemed to cower in fear at our laughter. My ego was getting the best of me. I made it to the river kayaking a few times that winter, but not near as many as in years past. Friday and Saturday evening were usually spent watching the WVU wrestling team do battle with other colleges. It was the kind of entertainment I was craving at the time. I know longer went to the MMA gym in Morgantown, and the wrestling coach never returned my calls about walking onto the team earlier in the year, so this was as close as I would get to a fight. It was exciting and captivating, but the matches only lasted 2 hours or so, so I had to find a way to spend the rest of my down time. I had a buddy in town who never seemed to be concerned with how crazy, and socially awkward I had become. We'll call him DC. We spent many weekends together, him, his girlfriend, and me. We spent many nights eating, smoking, and watching television on his couch. His girlfriend at the time kind of clashed with my conception of reality and harmonizing with the Great Spirit, but my friend took me in unconditionally so I never let her bother me. Instead I thought of her as quaint, and integral to our social dynamic. They were among the few I was able to call "friend."

That's when it was getting dangerous. I had friends in town, but I didn't feel comfortable around them for long periods of time, or they did not feel comfortable around me. There were those who I now know truly cared about me, but when your concept of reality is based around hallucinations, it's tough to talk any real sense to you, or have a regular friendship. I held on a little too tightly to the power of Wonder Falls, and the shape shifting. The trees continued to wear shaded patterns as they lined the ridges, and their personality seemed to be sending me encrypted messages. I thought they were doing Katie Jones' bidding.

I knew nothing aside from the fact that April was on the way. The blooming season was afoot, and it was captivating. The natural world was coming to life before me. All the wonder and power that was stored in those stems and roots all winter was transforming into beauty and amazement as the days became warmer and longer. I spent as much time as I could walking and mountain biking the trails that cut through the woods on the edge of town, and I spent some time camping at Wonder Falls by myself. When I felt overwhelmed by Morgantown I took to the woods, either Wonder Falls or the university forest near Coopers Rock. I found myself in either one of those wilds more often than I had hoped in the four years I spent in West Virginia.

As nature came to life, the level of communication I discovered between myself and plants while hunting in late archery laid stewing in my mind. The buds of the trees and plants gleamed with vivid definition and color. I believe Katie Jones had her flora spell-bound, and I wondered if I could spin my own words to bring the flora to life. One day I was walking on a trail, and a bud appeared half unraveled to me. I took a close look at it and pondered. I had a few lovely words in my mind that carried a constant meter and thwarting force and began spinning a spell. The definition and color of the leaf coming to life became more vivid, and the bud seemed to bloom before me, but as my spell came to a collection of words that housed Katie Jones' real name, depression sunk in. I thought if she was not here to enjoy the beauty at hand then what was the effort worth, and I let it be. I didn't quit talking to plants, but I thought that enchanting them was worthless without a lover by my side.

Enchanting the weather on the other hand was fair game. Rain to raise the rivers or sunshine to warm my shoulders was in high demand regardless of who was by my side. I believed the sun and clouds knew who I was, and they paid attention to me. If I stood out on my porch and longed for the sun with respectable posture and a clear mind, the skies would clear and the light would shine down on my world. If I raised smoke to the sky and looked at the horizon with disdain, clouds seemed to come and rain usually fell. It was ludicrous, but it happened with enough consistency for me to believe I could actually control the weather. It was dangerous. What I believed to be my arsenal of supernatural powers was growing. I didn't believe myself to be all that different from everyone else though. I thought others had the power to do the same but had not yet experienced the things to instill such knowledge on how to use those powers. As I tried to stay high every waking hour, Morgantown seemed to be an enchanted place. People seemed to appear as trolls and fairies as I walked the streets.

The authorities have powers of their own when it came to matters of reconnaissance and surveillance. As students and professors shape shifted, bent light, and spun enchanting words and ideas, the authorities appeared to try and keep our magic under wraps. They tapped into our computers, and phones, and iPods. They tapped into our cars, homes, and minds. I thought they were after me. I thought bigger fish were after me. I thought the CIA was watching my every move on satellite imagery, and they had men on the ground following me. There was an incident that backed my delusional belief. I was walking back to my apartment from class one morning that spring. It was a nice day. I thought I'd go for a walk. Just as I passed my apartment a police car pulled up in front of me and cut my path off. Two officers got out of the car, began asking me questions, and before I knew it, I was in handcuffs. I thought "They know I'm powerful. They're trying to bring me down." I don't think they had any real reason to put me in cuffs or detain me for the hour that I was in cuffs. They were just assholes. They called in paramedics to check my vitals then released me. I was furious and felt violated. I was in handcuffs for over 20 minutes just sitting on the sidewalk. It did wonders for my insanity.

Chapter 8: River Class

I spent all spring semester editing River Class. Proof reading and rewriting was my favorite pastime. I became enthralled with the work. It was exciting. Writing the original cut allowed me to relive the past 5 years of my life, the highs, the lows, and the meandering transitions. Once I got into editing, I became a little too proud of what I had produced. I could see the flaws in my writing, but those were overshadowed by the events they captured. I believed it to be the most raw and exciting account of my generation, the millennial college crowd. I wasn't satisfied with the story alone. It wasn't intelligent enough. It was simply raw and exciting. I hungered for delusional stimulation somewhere in my story. I worked over philosophy and literature until I had something that made the brain think a lot. A foreword to the book was produced. Then a chapter curtailing all the connections I was beginning to make between the supernatural and nature. This chapter was later cut out, and installed into the publication as the afterword. The chapter was going to be titled "La Paz" Spanish for "The Peace". I thought it was integral to the story, some account for connecting where I had been and where I was at the time. I later realized that it was a little too abstract to include it in the body of the book. I spent too much time working over other literature and picking my own brain to completely delete the work. I was proud of it. Today though, it's just a vivid reminder of how far out I had gone. There were truths in there and thought-provoking ideas, but I wouldn't call that piece of writing my best work.

Once the first round of editing was complete, I was on cloud nine. I thought I had a best seller. It just needed published. I was in the up-and-coming author's state of mind: "If I can just get one person to look at it, it will fly high." I talked to professors about getting it off the ground and began walking the trail. First I needed an agent. I contacted a few and the ones that did respond were not impressed. My head was big once the writing was done, and as I began to get feedback on my work, I just became angry with the professionals who didn't see the excitement and beauty in River Class that I did. I was getting more and more angry and bitter with the world week by week. I thought "My only hope is taking it straight to the top." I was going to hand-deliver the manuscript to The Oxford University Press in New York City myself.

Chapter 9: Cheat Fest

The spring semester at WVU ended, and I had two choices, either take the geology field trip out west or go to Cheat Fest. I barely had enough money for the trip, and I wanted to return to Johnstown and start working ASAP, so I chose Cheat Fest. Part of me wanted to go to see if I would cross paths with Katie Jones in some kind of heartfelt reunion. Part of me was there for the down-river race and the festival, and part of me was there to sell off my kayaking gear. The crack in my boat became unrepairable over winter as I attempted welding it shut. I used a butane torch and I told myself "Do it slowly, and it can be done. If you hurry, you'll ruin the boat." I didn't listen to my own advice and warped the plastic. I was hell-bent on running the down-river race on the Friday of the festival, though, so I borrowed a friends river runner. It was and old-school whitewater boat, a Dagger Crossfire. The hull design and ergonomics were different from mine, but I had the outlook that I was a good enough paddler to make the transition seamlessly.

I got to the campground early Friday. A few people were in the guide's campground, a few familiar faces from Ohiopyle. They let me camp there even though I hadn't work as a river guide in almost two years. I parked the Subaru, and hung a tarp and a tapestry for some privacy and protection from the wind. I also hung the big bucksaw I took camping the December prior. I had some idea about falling a few trees. Don't ask. I spent the afternoon smoking and taking in the sun then as afternoon approached evening, I began to get ready for the race. I had high hopes of winning the race. That was until I saw the wildwater boats, big long things with V-bottom hulls that cut through the water with speed.

There were between 70-100 boats at the starting line. The gun fired and everyone was off. I fell into the second half of the pack as we got through the first rapid, a class III named Decisions. I kept my pace, and didn't fall behind any further until we made it to Big Nasty. I usually run the wave-train, skirt the wave-hole at the bottom and eddy out on the bottom left. The race had my mind in a different gear though. I wanted to bomb the hole, and make my way down to the next rapid with a little speed. I hit the hole and flipped. I was upside down against the eddy-line trying to roll up. Things weren't working for me. Between me, the boat, and the river, I wasn't able to hit my roll. I swam and lost about 15 positions in the process. The level was around 3-3.25', mostly class III whitewater with a few relatively friendly class IV rapids. I did flip once more. I forget on which rapid, but once again I was unable to roll up. I bounced off rocks and was reacquainted with my boat on shore. It took a little while on the banks for me to regain strength, and I lost about another 20 positions. There wasn't much river left to paddle after that. I thought I was dead last when I took out at the Jenkinsburg Bridge, but to my surprise there were about 15 paddlers behind me.

That night I roamed the campground alone. My bass was in my car, but I thought that I'd be better off just walking with my pipe, and a jar of smoke, instead. Sure enough, I would eventually run into a band of hillbilly gypsies playing music, and guess what they didn't have? A bassist. Oh well, I smoked, and we smoked, and I did my part to amplify whatever energy was pervading through the airways in that campground. Eventually I made my way back to my tent, and fell asleep for the night. Saturday morning came, and I had already spent all the time I had intended to spend on the river that weekend. I gathered my gear, carried all of it over to the festival entrance, and put a "For Sale" sign on it. I sat there for about an hour. I managed to sell my spray-skirt, then shortly after I saw a girl in a flowered skirt, black halter top, 5'8" with curly black hair pulled back in a bun, sure enough it was Katie

Jones. I sat there and said out loud to myself, "That's the last time I'll ever see her" with a little emptiness in my voice.

Then I picked myself up, and walked after the girl and her friend. I had only seen Katie twice since Cheat Fest the year prior. Once in the Library at WVU where we had kind of an awkward conversation, and once in town she rode past me on her bicycle. That was it. I'm not sure what I hoped for when I saw her in May 2011. I caught up with her near the porta-johns, fittingly. She was happy to see me as I was her. We hugged, and I leaned in for a kiss. I was determined but she wiggled away from it as I said "Let me do this just once before I die!" with a bit of laughter in my voice. I laid one on her cheek. She laughed, and I let her go. We made small talk about our plans for the near future, and when she told me she was moving to California for good, I was a little heartbroken. I don't know what I expected from her at the time. It should have been nothing more than a hug and smile, but I was still deeply attracted to the girl who was 4 years my senior. We parted. As I walked in front of a police officer in front of the stage, I pulled out a joint in shear spite, and fired it up. I was getting angrier and angrier by the minute. Katie Jones and I left the festival grounds around the same time. She and her friend were getting in her truck, and they saw me walking back to my camp. I looked to see if she noticed me. She did and yelled out as loud as she could.

"I love you!"

I shook my head with disappointment as she fired up her truck and drove away. By the time I made it back to my tent I was furious. I pulled out my knife, and cut down all the tarps. A guide I used to work with came over and kicked me out because of it. I packed up my things then headed back to Johnstown. Somewhere around the West Virginia-Pennsylvania state line my creek boat flew off my roof. I heard it hit the road behind me, and with its unrepairable crack ,I left it behind and just kept motoring along.

So the semester was over, and I was in Johnstown once again, a place I had hoped to distance myself from. Most of the bullshit I came across was fed to me elsewhere; Morgantown, Cove Forge, Cheat Fest, etc. etc. I just believed if I could put Johnstown behind me, memories of all those other unsavory places would be forgotten with it. For the most part I created my own problems; drug use, attempted suicide, schizophrenia. They were all factors of my character, character conditioned by where I lived and who I lived with. I was dealing with a lot of problems, problems that were reflections of the man I had become. I wanted to forget that person and start life new, start in a place that offered romance, success, and understanding. It's hard to start over without a little money to get on your feet or at least a little money for a train ticket out of hell. My funds were near zero. That Monday I went on the job hunt. The first place I looked for work was where I found employment for most of my young life, a landscaping company. The boss didn't need me so I looked up a few other landscaping companies. Nobody seemed too interested in hiring, so I went home and fixed my head. A few long drags on my pipe put my psyche where I desired it to be. Oddly enough where I desired it to be and where it best fit into the world were not the same.

I was by myself at my parents' house. Meditating in the sunlight seemed like the best way to find peace. I sat on the lawn facing the late morning sun, and closed my eyes. I tried to go somewhere. That somewhere was no reflection of any place I had been before. I had no concept of that ideal place I longed to be. My brain was wry and my mind sunk into all the situations of my past. I quickly went from peace to rage. I wanted to blame someone. My father seemed like the best target, as even the most innocent are. I pulled my hunting knife and slashed one of the tires on his pickup truck. It was retribution for raising me to be the rascal I had become. I got in my car and drove to a friend's house. We hiked and played guitar all afternoon. When the sun started getting low in the sky, I decided to go home and face the music. The question from my parents was simple: did I know how it happened? At first I was going to lie my way out of it. Could they really discredit me and call my bluff? So, I answered with deference. Then my conscience got the best of me. I admitted to putting my steel into the rubber. Harsh words and actions followed. I didn't know what to do. I left my keys on the kitchen table, grabbed my bag and headed for the hills. I spent the next week living in the woods, occasionally showing up at the house to eat and shower. I was a vagabond. I had no regards for the law. I wanted to unchain myself from humanity, and society. Both had left a bitter taste in my mouth. All that I thought I needed was sunlight, food, and water. Some nights I spent leaning up against a tree, wrapped in a blanket, waking often. I would wake as morning twilight set in, and as the sky turned a lighter shade of blue, I tried not to become impatient in waiting for the sun to rise. When its rays crested the hilltop, the light and warmth filled me with delight. The days passed and I laid about and organized my camp. I would get restless as the day passed and go for walks. The birds kept me company. I listened to their songs, and tried not to think too much. I had distanced myself from society and humanity in the external, physical sense, but mentally and emotionally I still had much anger and angst.

Thursday rolled around, and I knew a few vendors would be setting up for the Stonycreek River Rendezvous that coming weekend. I threw a blanket, a hat, and my canteen into a daypack and hoofed it a few miles down to Greenhouse Park. The fields and country roads put my mind at peace while my feet motored along. I was right! Vendors were afoot! We set up some tents and gear, and I relished the moment. The whitewater community had become my family and support group over time. They listened to and accepted me. There was never judgement, well almost never. When I pulled my knife and started slashing ropes at Cheat Fest two weeks prior, there was judgement. They made me take a look at what I was doing and understand it. I did. I didn't question the authority of the whitewater community. I just felt a little more disgusted with who I had become. I felt as though I was bound to live on the run, hopping from festival to festival, and never finding sustained peace and happiness.

That night I slept on a park bench next to the fire in Greenhouse Park. I woke early and stirred with the rising sun. A local paddler gave me a ride back to my house, and we made arrangements to gather some smoke for the weekend. I arrived at my house just as my parents were leaving for work. I thought "Hmm, this festival would be a great opportunity to do some writing." I had all my work saved on my flashdrive. I packed my computer and my electric bass guitar as I was told there would be a slot for me and a friend to play a short set at the festival Saturday night. I didn't have a boat so I didn't bother packing my river gear. I waited for my ride with nearly everything ready that I wanted for the weekend. The only piece missing was my flash drive. I searched high and low for it, but it was nowhere to be found. "My Dad hid it!" I thought. "He never wants me to publish my book and ascend out of this shit-hole!" I couldn't contain the rage I felt. I walked in the house and grabbed the biggest, heaviest thing I could get out the door. It was a 70 lb. ceramic crock. I walked out the door with it, and hurled it through the driver's window of my dad's pickup. When I heard the glass shatter I couldn't believe what I had done. I couldn't stand to face the music from my family once more. I walked inside and called the police on myself. I hid my pipe in the woods and sat and waited for the cops to show up. Sure enough, after about 15 minutes two cruisers came rolling up the street. I sat in the driveway with my pack and my bass guitar. They asked what happened, and I gave some bullshit story about how I came home and found the truck like that, then I retracted my statement, and told them what really happened. When they tried putting the cuffs on me, I stood up and walked away. They tackled me to the ground and called in an ambulance. The paramedics arrived and put me in a straight-jacket. I figured I was about to spend the rest of my days inside padded walls. I screamed at the paramedic. It was the first time I was ever in a straight-jacket. It's unbelievably worse than handcuffs. The level of restraint sends the mind into a state of fear, a fear on complete uncertainty of where you are headed, who will have control over you, and how they will 'care' for you. I was under lock and key with no way out.

Chapter 10: Mental Hospital

The whole ride to the hospital I kept thinking "This is the end of the line." I had no idea what to expect, but I didn't see a way out. I felt hopeless. Once I finally got to the hospital they wheeled me in and strapped me to a bed. I was in some kind of staging room. The white walls and white tile floors were sterile. Sterile aromas pervaded the atmosphere, and the spirit of the whole place felt synthetic. The hospital bed they strapped me in was hard and flat. I felt like a prisoner. The rigid contrast between the excitement of the morning, and the restraint of the afternoon left me in shambles. Every time I tried to think about freedom, I got worked up and saw nothing but a dark abyss of future. I laid there for a few hours and eventually was able to put the magnitude of the situation out of my head for a little while. I just kept telling myself this was temporary and I would be released. I just had to relax and keep it together until the doctors got bored with me, and then I would be free to go. How little did I know.

After two or three hours, my mother showed up. When she asked what happened I snapped. I burst out with hopeless rage, screaming about how badly I hated my life.

Katie Jones, school, and distance from my friends and family had me in a dark place. In that moment, I thought things would always be as bleak as they were that day. I was afraid of being alone and working hard labor for peanuts the rest of my life. I didn't want to explain what my problem was. I didn't know what it was. I had to overcome. I just wanted to exclaim that I had problems, problems that appeared impossible to face at this point. I thought publishing River Class was the one way to fix everything, and that was beginning to present challenges. After my outburst, they unstrapped me from the table, strapped me to a wheelchair, and took me to the seventh floor, the mental ward.

The elevator door opened, and I was wheeled in. We went up. Then, the doors opened again. Before me was a lobby where doors had to be unlocked before entering the mental ward. Three hallways converged to a T where the reception desk laid. Behind the reception desk, nurses talked to each other and other patients. The halls were dark. There was a window at the end of the west wing. The east wing was punctuated with a small sitting room and a containment room, a white-walled room fitted with a bed and restraints. The south wing had an arts-and-crafts room at the end of the hall, along with a locked door that lead to a stairwell.

There was little natural light in the seventh floor. The dark green industrial carpet was slightly illuminated by fluorescent lights. This was way different from Cove Forge and even a little different from the dual diagnosis unit in Clarion. There were about thirty patients, every one of them dealing with various mental health issues. Some patients were in better shape than others. None of them looked happy. As soon as I got there I felt trapped and had the feeling that the others felt trapped too. Unrealistic conversations filled the air. Faces made expressions of broken wills. Eyes pierced my being, demanding validation of others' minds, bodies, and spirits. Before long I saw a doctor. They sat me in an office, and I waited on her to enter. She did, and shut the door behind her. She asked the usual questions.

"Did I use any drugs? If so what were they? Was I allergic to anything? Did I have any pre-existing conditions?"

Then after all my questions they made me empty my pockets into a ziplock bag. Sure enough, when I did there was the flash drive I was certain my father hid from me. I about boiled over right then and there. This whole headache could have been avoided if only I checked my pants pockets thoroughly. I overlooked the obvious and was blindsided by a most heinous affair. I walked out of the office, and felt like part of the patients who were held on the seventh floor. I was one of these captives.

After my reception a nurse approached me. It was around 6:30 in the evening and I had missed dinner. The nurse gave me a menu and told me I could order anything I wanted. I saw steak sandwiches on there, and ordered two. As I waited for my food, I sat in the middle-sized room out of the three. This one was dark with big comfortable chairs and a table in the middle with boxes of puzzles on it. I sat there with another man who was getting ready to be released the next day. On the outside world I would have ignored the man, maybe even made a negative judgement, but this instance was different. Even though he looked unkept with long dirty-blond hair, we were wearing the same shoes. He wore a black-and-gold shirt, and shoes that inferred an attraction to urban culture. He spoke with a hint of fear in his voice. His eyes looked uncertain. We talked to each other, but few words were shared. As I waited for my food, I wondered if I would get out in time to play the gig at the Stonycreek Rendezvous. It weighed heavy on my mind. I felt like I had become such an integral part of the Stonycreek River that I needed to shed personal vibrations upon all who had come to paddle and party in our little watershed. I thought it was a way to transcend my reality, my problems, and become a star. It may have even offered an opportunity for publicity for River Class!

The Rendezvous stewed in my brain. Before long, my food came and I ate. Then, they showed me to my room. It was sterile, white walls, a white floor, and a typical hospital bed. A big window laid to the right of the bed. The place felt unnatural, synthetic, and brewed anxiety. I was emotionally spent by this point and wanted to lay down and forget about the day. My mother brought me a few changes of clothes earlier in the day. I showered and changed, then laid in my bed as it got dark outside. I can't remember whether or not they gave me medication, nor If I slept the whole night through, but I did manage to chill out a little bit. The following day was Saturday. The doctors didn't come in to evaluate patients on Saturdays. I wouldn't be released. I thought I was letting hundreds of people down by being locked up on Rendezvous weekend. The festival had become so crucial to my lifestyle over the past few years that I couldn't imagine being kept from it. It was heartbreaking. I became upset and slipped into a bit of a dither. I saw the fabric of my life slowly unravelling before me. I was on the way down.

That weekend, while I became familiar with the walls around me, delusions of grandeur had become strong. I thought men should bow down before me because where I've been, what I've been through, and my written account of it all. I still thought I had supernatural powers, but that was still mostly unseen by others. When Monday came around, I was finally seen by a psychiatrist. It was an Asian man who was vaguely familiar. Eventually I pieced the memories together and it was the same man who shipped me out of Somerset Hospital, and into Cove Forge a year earlier. He could see something was off about me. Maybe it was a generalization he made about all of his patients. He began his version of what was going on in my mind. To him I was simply psychotic, and needed to be pumped full of drugs. They began with an anti-psychotic, Risperdal, for the first week of my stay. I didn't become any more mentally stable. It would be weeks before anything seemed to help. The medication and walls raised my anxiety. I worked around it, and tried socializing with the staff, and distanced myself from the patients. I didn't want to make any connections with insanity, but I couldn't overcome reality.

Every day I saw the doctor. Everyday he told me how I had no self-control and needed medication. He was the warden, and I was one of his prisoners, and a repeat offender at that. I didn't make a good appearance before him by winding up in the mental ward of two different hospitals within a year and a half under his 'care'. The walls were hard enough to become familiar with. At least in other facilities I could go outside and smoke a cigarette a couple times a day. Not here I was on the 7th floor 24/7. This was the longest I have ever had to be locked up indoors in my entire life. Between the containment and condescending opinion of my psychiatrist, I felt the crushing blow of the system. There was nothing I could do about it. I was enraged, but I had to bite my tongue and curb my impulses day after day. I became friendly with the windows. There were a few that let in a sliver of sunlight for a few minutes a day, and I longed for it. Most patients walked the halls or sat in the biggest sitting-room. Conversations were sparse and obscure. I refused to make friends most of the time. Opinions were radical and sometimes irrational. The mental condition of the patients ranged from depressed and mildly delusional to completely psychotic. They looked fearful, or deranged, or impulsive, or traumatized. The professionals tried to ignore and condescend upon patients. This is the worst action that can be taken towards such people because doing so destroys any pre-existing concepts about compassion in humanity. That is all that a psychotic person has to hold on to, compassion. When that is stolen, there is no good that exists in the mind, just feelings of hate and ideas of retribution. The doctor was stealing my ideals of compassion, and as he did I drifted farther and farther from reality.

By the end of the week doctors had scheduled a meeting between me, my parents, and some professionals. When the staff found out, they were all encouraging. All of the nurses said I would be out in no time. The meeting was held in the cafeteria on the seventh floor. Three or four of us sat around a table and talked about options. The Asian doctor wasn't one of them. In my mind there was only one option: release me then and there. I thought that was the plan. They talked about how long I needed to be kept at the hospital, then what would happen when I was released. I became furious. I insulted the professionals, cursed, and threw a chair. I was going to be on the seventh floor for a while. I tried to curb my rage from inside my room for the rest of the day. I could only remember being *that angry* once before in my life. At that moment I realized I had no control over my fate. Whatever the professionals decided was exactly how things were going to play out. I wish the psychiatrists could see the good in my soul that the nurses saw from me everyday. I was upset that my parents didn't do more to extract me from that prison, but looking back on it, I can't blame them for letting the system have its way with me. I was a loose cannon at home. I couldn't avoid confrontation, and felt the urge to destroy everything in sight without any instigation. I was perceiving emotions and expressions from other people that didn't exist. I thought everyone was out to get me; society, my family, now the professionals on the seventh floor of Conemaugh Hospital.

My second week passed slowly and my anxiety constantly increased. I was contained, never allowed to step foot outside and feel the wind in my face, or sun on my shoulders. Nature had always been my greatest pleasure in life, greater than women, drugs, money or entertainment. It was my release. I felt spiritually connected with it. Now I was being withheld from enjoying it even on the most subtle level, and my psyche was paying the price. The longer I spent in the mental ward, the further down-hill my mind went. Locking up the mentally ill just creates an environment to facilitate mental illness. By doing that, you eliminate all references, and relationships to reality. Crazy gets crazier. I couldn't handle the Risperdal anymore and asked for something different. They put me on lithium next. The whole time on lithium I felt spaced out and brain dead, completely sedated. It felt like the day after drinking an entire bottle of whiskey. I hated the way my brain was processing information, and quit taking lithium, cold turkey. I drank a bunch of water to try to vomit up the pills. Bad idea. I woke in the middle of the night, and my arms, legs, and stomach were cramping horribly. It was hard to breathe. I was vomiting violently, and felt like I had to shit in the worst way. I didn't know what was going on. I thought maybe my appendix burst that night. It didn't, and by this point I was fed up with the medication routine. I began refusing what they suggested the next night. Still, I was forced to take something to sedate me. They shoved a needle filled with olanzapine in my asscheek. It wasn't bad, and after three nights of the injection I became used to it. Best of all, there were no side-affects. When I started welcoming the injection, nurses noticed, and offered me the medication in an orally dissolving tablet, Zyprexa Zydys. If taking it regularly without objection meant I got out of the mental ward any quicker I was down.

As time went on in the mental ward, my state of mind went from bad to worse. I thought there was something special about me, namely, knowledge and power when I came in. Now all the delusional mysticism I once believed to be at my will was my handicap. By the end of the third week of my stay, it was no rare occurrence for me to drop to my knees, and cry, wail, and plead for salvation

on the spot, as the voices in my head spoke dark,
intimidating messages of hate and disregard. That wasn't
all that was black-balling me. My ego rubbed the Asian
psychiatrist the wrong way. When I sat before him with
either an air of grandeur about me, or expressions of anger
towards him, he would tell me "You leave me no choice
but to send you to Torrence (state mental hospital). Your
parents don't want you home." He always delivered the
lines with a shitty grin and instigating eyes behind his little
frameless glasses.

    I thought he was lying, but over time I realized my
parents didn't want me back at the house, at least not until I
was mentally stable, and they were willing to wait as long
as it took to reach that state. I thought the whole world was
fucking me over, and my anger grew, day by day. The
second week was long, and I thought it would soon be over.
Soon I would breathe fresh air again. No, towards the end
of the second week I received a court-order, hand-
delivered, stating that I had to stay for an additional 7 to 20
days. When I read those words my heart dropped. Every
day was a challenge, and that challenge was about to be
prolonged. I fought to hold on to any comfort I could find.
The place was effixiating, and I had at least another week
before being released from the 7th floor. I didn't know if I
could make it. I began hearing voices, and feeling

sensations that sent me into hysteria. My perception was amiss, badly. My concept of reality was paying the price. I heard language that expressed desires to keep me locked up until I committed suicide, real and imaginary. I called out telepathically to my friends to save me, and no one responded. I even collected the fax number for the mental ward in hopes that the president of the United States would grant me clemency. I began socializing with the other patients. Everyone felt sympathy for the others on that floor. I stood beside an older man suffering from depression and we gazed the window at the end of the west wing together. I felt hopeless and helpless, but at least I had someone to share those moments with. My bed shifted from room to room. Roommates changed. Some rooms were sterile. Some were carpeted, and a bit more homely. I spent hours in bed thinking over semantics and logic about how to rationalize heaven from within that hell. There was a state of mind I tried to achieve, but I always felt clenched within the grasp of the professionals. I had three different roommates and changed rooms twice while I was in the mental ward. My roommates got my mind off detainment. One was a homeless black guy. He was older, and I told him tales from Native American cultures. He enjoyed it. When I looked at that man's face he looked poised for punishment, but was unsure who or where it would come from. He looked like a man constantly trying to weather the storm. I had a roommate who claimed to receive a garbage bag full of marijuana from a friend who was days away from going to jail. I laughed and even salivated at the thought. On the third Saturday on the seventh floor, a patient was appointed to my room. He had a family, and a drinking problem. Like me, he burst out in a fit of rage and checked himself in after tearing the fan off the kitchen cieling. When he arrived I was getting irritated by one of the patients on the seventh floor, and I told my new roommate not to ask me anything and I wouldn't ask him anything. I had enough of my own problems. I didn't need to hear about his, and I sure as hell didn't need his opinion about my problems. I would figure a way out of all of this.

We received three meals a day, a snack before night-time medication, and hot beverages twice a day. My roommate with the garbage bag full of weed always talked with a bit of tempted desire when they announced it was time for hot beverages. It was a release. Coffee, tea, or cocoa was served, and you waited for the drink to cool, then slowly sipped, feeling the comfort in its flavor and temperature. Aside from meals and hot beverages, there was craft time for an hour immediately before lunch, and an old acoustic guitar floated around. By the third week of my stay I attended craft time daily. Oragami, coloring, and drawing seemed to drain away a little bit of time. No hour was any easier to pass than another. The mornings were slow. The evenings and afternoons were slow. The nights were slow, and my mind raced every hour, provoking my heart to do the same. My nerves were shot by the third week and I had developed a few plans to escape; one through the door, one through the window, and one in handcuffs. On Memorial Day, there would be distractions in a nearby park, and I planned to run out through the front lobby when the breakfast trays were carted in. I made it through the first set of doors, but when I got to the elevator, an older nurse stood between me and a way out. I couldn't throw the woman out of my way. I didn't have it in me. One plan that I thought over day after day was sprinting down the west wing, crashing through window at the end of the hall, and falling seven stories to my death. Thankfully I didn't stay that long. Another option in my mind was to physically assault someone, and be sent to prison. At least there I would get to go outside for an hour every day. Things were looking bleak. I had no reality, just fear and restlessness.

The nurses looked on with sympathy, and even confronted me. They told me I looked incredibly worse than I did when I arrived, and they would ask the doctor to release me. Quarantining the mind resolves nothing. It only makes things worse. There was no practice of mental health that I could see in that mental ward. I was human just like the many others that came in, and were released while I had to stay. A healthy life involves involvement in either society or nature, not removing an individual from every natural interaction that accumulates to the sum we call life. The doctor must have listened to the nurses, and began expressing pleasure with me for agreeing to take the medication regularly.

Shortly before the point of no return, some social workers from Somerset County came to the hospital and offered me placement into a 'Long Term Structured Rehabilitation Facility'. It was a low stress environment where I was required to take medication, and live under the supervision of social workers with a handful of other patients. I would also be seen by a psychiatrist once a month, and was required to stay there for at least 90 days. It was the only way out that I saw. I took it and ran. I spent 33 days total on the seventh floor, and by the time I was released, my vitamin-D levels had been so depleted from the lack of sunshine that my teeth were working loose in my skull. I wasn't able to make sense of that place. I was kept under close watch, which was foreign. I was not allowed to go outside, which was foreign. And, I had no clue what the future held, which was foreign. I had no intentions of ever getting used to that place. It was supposed to be temporary but as the second week turned into the third, then the fourth, I feared it would be permanent, especially when the doctor kept telling me that he was going to send me to the state mental hospital. Watching Katie Jones kiss the short, fat, red-headed man at Cheat Fest was bad, but the seventh floor of Conemaugh Hospital was hell. The uncertainty of my future was the worst part as I lived my life from within the mental ward. On June 16th a social worker from Somerset picked me up from Conemaugh Hospital in a minivan. I was released, and we were on our way to Trilogy House.

Chapter 11: Trilogy House

June 16th was a cloudy day. Being able to step
outside and reconnect with reality was unbelievably good.
It was great! I never understood what freedom meant until
I was locked up for 33 days then released from the seventh
floor of Conemaugh Hospital. The atmosphere I was
confronted with was average, dreary spring weather in the
Laurel Highlands. The social worker who picked me up
asked if I wanted to stop anywhere for tobacco. I was
thrilled at the thought of tossin' in a chew. Freedom at last!
We made the 40 minute drive from Johnstown to Somerset,
and when I arrived at the Long Term Structured
Rehabilitation facility, it began to rain. The place was
called Trilogy House. That's exactly what it was, a house,
like in a regular neighborhood. The driveway was tucked
back into a woodlot. The yard was bordered by a chain-
link fence, and there was a back porch with a roof and
chairs. I arrived near the top of the hour. It was smoke
break. Almost all of the patients were sitting on the back
porch smoking cigarettes, just watching the rainfall. Before
I arrived I was told I could be released before the 90 days
were up if the doctor thought I was healthy enough. I

thought for sure this new doctor would see what I saw in myself, and release me in three or four weeks.

I said a quick hello to the 5 or 6 people sitting outside as I made my way into Trilogy House. I had my clothes in a garbage bag, and when I entered, a social worker showed me my room. There were two beds, but I didn't have a roommate. The carpet was worn, brown berber. The walls of my bedroom were painted light blue. The bed was a twin with a plastic cover around the mattress. I placed my clothes in a dresser, and my toiletries and a few shirts in the closet. Then I walked outside and started learning names and faces. There were two boys a year or two younger than me, both in their early 20's. One was heavy-set and one was a rock and roller with long blonde hair. One seemed to doubt himself a lot, and yearned for validation from others. The other boy seemed pretty self-confident. I would later find out the self-confident one, we'll call him Dice, was diagnosed with schizophrenia, and the other boy had bipolar disorder. Both could play guitar, but Dice could really shred. There were two women there who I felt the need to get to know as well. One was in her mid thirties and the other in her late twenties. Both were pretty, and like the boys, one had bipolar and the other schizophrenia. I became friends with all four, the two boys and two women. There were a few other patients who were middle-aged or older, but I didn't feel the need to develop any personal relationships with them.

For the first time in my life I didn't feel like I was going through this fight alone. I was living with people who were on the same path, sobriety, medication, and self-awareness. The place had a positive energy, and we all fed off each other. The girls got catty with each other once or twice while I was there, but everyone felt connected. Dice and I jammed some of the time, and the rest of the time was spent talking, or just fooling around. I spent time alone in my bedroom too, but I wasn't a recluse, and I didn't feel the need to keep myself guarded. Most of us had a drug addiction at one time or another, whether it was prescription drugs, heroine, meth, LSD, or marijuana. That was a conversation piece when social workers weren't looking over our shoulders. It was our dirty little pleasure. When we talked about it, we got excited and giddy, but life felt good at Trilogy House, and I don't think any one of else really had a desire to get high. We were with friends, and our responsibilities were minimal. The girls had their guilty pleasure too. Both were strippers at one point in time, and they would talk about it in front of me and Dice on occasion. Their words were saucy and spoken with pouty lips and devilish eyes. Everyone was very careful about the words they said or what they talked about because we were kept under close watch. We were there to get better, not talk about fast lifestyles, but when we felt rebellious questionable memories surfaced. Talk of intoxicating adventures came to life, and the four of us were not in short supply. Yet, the idea of Trilogy House was to focus on the positive. Talk about healthy things and take pleasure in innocent happiness. We were trying to build habits that would perpetuate the good in life. The circumstance reminded us why we were there. We had come to the end of the line and needed a change. Most of us were on our final straw. If we didn't fix our problems that time around we, wouldn't get another chance. Every one of us were court-ordered to be there, and we all took advantage of the opportunity to make an effort to fix the problems in our lives, or at least the problems we could fix.

I think the idea of Trilogy House LTSR was to establish a controlled, low-stress environment so everyone could overcome their problems. Every person there seemed to have gone through very traumatic experiences at some point in their life, and faced those tribulations with a chemical imbalance to complicate matters further. This was a chance to sit back and face today, and we faced today. We didn't turn to sex or drugs to get away from our problems like the four of us have done in the past. For too long we pushed our problems to the backs of our minds, and they accumulated into an overwhelming collection of hard and ugly. Drugs coddle the mind, and by indulging in the feel-good-moment, you quite maturing mentally and emotionally. That doesn't condition your spirit to overcome obstacles and become stronger. You cripple yourself by not facing your problems, and lock yourself into a stalemate. We were learning how to overcome that incredible accumulation of problems in our lives. We were given a chance to resolve our issues in hopes to return to civilization, and be productive members of society. "Today" at Trilogy House was not overwhelming.

We had group therapy every morning for two hours. We went for short walks every day. We had chores, helped cook dinner, and occasionally went for coffee or ice cream or something like that. Trilogy House was quite sane compared to the seventh floor of Conemaugh Hospital. I had no problem making social connections with most of the other patients here. I spent most of the time hanging out with Dice. He was the closest friend I had at a time when I learned the most about myself. He had the highs and the lows in his past just like me, from being a manager at a high-class restaurant to a homeless drug addict on the streets of Los Angeles. I told him my stories, and he told me his.

We could relate, and were swept away by each other's stories. He had life, color, and character in his face, and I was regaining it in mine. We had a grip on reality at Trilogy House. We weren't tormented by society, and we were working to calm our own minds. We weren't high on drugs. We just talked, played cards, and picked bass and guitar together. Before Trilogy House, reality was kind of elusive. Dice told me how he waited in a field one night for aliens to pick him up, and carry him away. He knew how crazy that sounded and we both laughed. I divulged a few of my delusions with him, and we probably laughed at those as well. We were allowed to build fires in the fire-ring in the yard on evenings, and we spent many a dusk around the fire reflecting, or immersing ourselves in deep conversation. One night we sat silently around the fire, and out of nowhere Dice said to me, "*I don't hate myself.*" It was a bold statement. Most people never have to strive to achieve that reality, or even contemplate such a decision. His statement stole me. I thought about my journey, and I agreed with him. I was working towards accepting myself. I'm not sure if I truly loved and accepted myself at that moment, but I wasn't angry with who I was and what I have become. At one point both of us hated ourselves. That wasn't who we were that day, and it felt good to share that moment with Dice. The strife for sanity involves understanding how to love yourself. Then, and only then, can you love another. Loving yourself involves making good decisions about your well-being. The years leading up to that summer were nothing but a long line of bad decisions. The day I graduated high school I began smoking marijuana every day. By the summer of 2011 I was almost constantly stoned. I never seemed to pursue women who wanted me in the same way I wanted them. And there was kayaking; it's good for the soul, but can definitely wear the nerves thin, especially after seeing your life flash before your eyes a few times from below the surface of the water.

After that night I began picking apart my relationships; my relationships with myself, my friends, my family, nature, and society. Katie Jones weighed heavy on my mind. It took some time before I could think about her, peacefully. Usually thoughts and memories of her just made me mad from the way she treated me, and how I failed to make her love me the way I loved her. There was so much history in the short time we knew each other. The night we spent in the Blue Moose coffee shop while I was tripped out on LSD a little over a year earlier made me think of her in a way I never thought of a woman before. I believed we were destined to be renegades, and she would be my mate. I would be Clyde and she my Bonnie as we chased adventure in nature, and in mystical psychedelic-fallacies. Eventually I came to the epiphany that she was *only a girl*. I told myself that every day until understood and believed it. Even after that I still felt hollow. It wasn't because I missed Katie, but there was a piece missing from my life.

About two weeks after I arrived, I saw the doctor. He came every Tuesday after supper, and everyone saw him on a monthly cycle. My week was the last Tuesday of the month. Going into Trilogy House, my diagnosis was depression. I thought I had bipolar disorder and post-traumatic stress disorder. After the incident at Wonder Falls I felt constant tension, isolation, and bewilderment. I longed for a companion to help carry the burden. Code Blue at Cove Forge left my mind far beyond the bounds of reality. Between that, the LSD, mushrooms, and fasting, my perception had become nothing but hallucinations. I couldn't conceptualize reality because I couldn't accurately perceive reality… schizophrenia at its finest. I needed help far more than I knew. That first session with the doctor, he could see emptiness and hopelessness in my eyes. I was far from all the balls and hot-air that I once was. The young man that doctor looked at was broken, and had no idea how to move forward. At one point during our meeting, in a low dismal voice I said to him, "You understand intelligent people." It was half a question, half a declaration, and was said without ever making eye-contact. Initially he took offense as he didn't clearly hear what I said, or see the expression in my eyes. When I repeated it looking him in the face, he began to understand a little more of who I was, and where I was at. After two sessions with the doctor my diagnosis changed from depression to schizophrenia. He believed I didn't have PTSD, but even to this day when I think about those moments I spent on the brink of life and death, I get tense and uneasy. It happens more than it should. When I found out my diagnosis, I didn't fight, argue or deny it. I welcomed it and addressed it with diligence, determined to make the most of my life. For too long I didn't believe I needed help, and I'm not sure anyone really knew how to help me until that point.

Things were changing within me as I readjusted to life after the mental ward. I felt improved. I was a little surprised by the latest diagnosis, but this doctor never cornered me, or condescended upon me. I respected his expertise, as he respected me, and I let him into all the fears and delusions in my head. I gained insight on how my psyche was flawed. Accepting his opinion was crucial. Had I disagreed, I would have stayed in that place until I accepted it. It was a chance to face my problems, head on. And by this point, I had no fear of that.

I did what I could, but I still felt empty. Then, one Sunday morning I rose early. Some of the patients were getting ready to go to church, and they asked if I wanted to join them. I already had a spiritual aspect to my life, and wasn't all that interested in hearing about God and Jesus, but I wanted to get out of the house for a little bit. I went and I listened to the priest in that church. In that holy place, a somber peace, a reverence came over me. Before Trilogy House, I believed I was some great spirit of the woods and rivers. My perception was so skewed that it all seemed to bend at my will, and I thought I had some supernatural power over it all. I thought Katie Jones and I were destined to be a storied duo among hippies, riverfolk and natural mystics. I thought we would run ramped until Armageddon, and our world turned back to the spirit world.

That first Sunday morning sitting in church for the first time in many years opened my eyes to an aspect of spirituality and divinity that I had long turned away from. There was spirit in the room, and it was calm, and comforting. I was intrigued, and went back to church the following Sunday. After two or three weeks of attendance, church, and God, and Christ made me feel like a part of the sum-whole. Before that I always felt like the sum of the parts. I continued to go to church. Sobriety and religion helped me piece together all the things that were beyond my control. I felt safe, happy, and snuggly-fit into creation as a believer in God. Jesus was the savior I was trying to become when I was mentally ill. Before I started going to church again, I thought a savior needed to be daring, but in truth Jesus was. He suffered hunger and the pains of death. He performed miracles. He healed and rose the dead. He was God in the form of a man, doing everything a man might be able to do, and somethings only God himself could accomplish. I found out that if I left all the hard decisions up to God, good would prevail. My belief in God and Christ became something tangible. It was a consciousness and an energy that filled me and made me whole. Such a vast emptiness opened in my soul over the years as I grew further and further away from my religion. That emptiness closed as I became filled with the Holy Spirit. Returning to it was like breathing new life into me. I had hope for the first time in a long time. God took me higher than drugs ever did. In August I began getting over-night, home-visitation on the weekends. I rose every Sunday morning and went to Church with my mother. Religion brought us close and I thrived on the strength it delivered. I was hungry for worship every week.

For what seemed like my entire life, I was angry; angry with myself, and angry with those closest to me. Christianity taught me many things, but the most valuable was forgiveness. I learned how to forgive myself and I learned how to forgive everyone who ever did me wrong. I went from telling myself that Katie Jones was *'just a girl'* to forgiving her for all the grief she caused me. I forgave my family for any wrong they may have ever done me, and I forgave myself for every poor, bull-headed decision I ever made. I finally found harmony. There was balance in my life. I wasn't at wit's end trying to decipher who held the power, or how I could hold the most. I just had balance between mind, body, and spirit. There was no need for the excess stimulation that I had chased for so long. That's what brought me down in the first place

By the time I was released from Trilogy House, I was attending church every Sunday. I was happy just to be alive, and sobriety wasn't nearly as painful as I once thought it to be. I felt no need to get high. The pleasure laid in simply being alive. I had lived through so much that life tasted sweeter than I ever believed it could. I was happy without Katie Jones. Jesus was my soul-mate.

Sometime in July of that summer, I went back and made a second round of edits to River Class while I was still in Trilogy House. I revised one chapter every day on the days I did not have home-visitation. After taking a sober look at what I had written, I finally saw how stony and delusional my ideas and language became over time. I was out there, and my story showed it. I don't believe anyone would have understood what I was trying to say throughout most of the story if I didn't take another look at the book after the smoke cleared. That was the big thing. I got away from drugs and social stress for such a long time that sanity finally restored itself. Religion helped. Maybe it was the strongest factor in my recovery, or at least the strongest factor in finding harmony, but I needed a few months away from excitement and punishment to restore a concept of life and reality that held truth and accuracy. As summer approached fall, I had begun to get stronger and healthier. I had control of my life for the first time in a long time. I knew what I wanted and how to get it. The future looked bright. I was released in early October.

Chapter 12: Resurrection

I was released from Trilogy House on October 11th, 2011. I went back to work for the landscaping company immediately. I was cutting grass with a wry guy who had a short temper. He worked hard, and we worked well together. We cooperated. That's more than I can say about some of the people I've worked with in the past. There are two things that breed success. Cooperation is one. The other is the ability to communicate knowledge. It's been said that knowledge is power, but it's only powerful if you can communicate that knowledge to other people so they understand. For a long time, I had accurate, in-depth ideas, but for most of that time I was not able to communicate my thoughts. Rehabilitation opened the door for me to develop that ability, and condition it into a well-oiled machine. I had clarity, and even in that environment of manual-labor, that clarity made work easier. I needed hard work for those first few weeks back in society. I put on 35 pounds while I was in rehab. I ate a lot, and didn't move very much. It added up, and for the first time in my life I had a gut. Cutting grass and shoveling dirt wasn't enough to get rid of it though. I had a medicine ball, and began working out with it for 30 minutes every-other day.

Between the exercise and my job, I found liberation that had been eluding me for too long.

There was a day in my youth when my soul cried for labor. Over time, that vanished, and even the most enjoyable of jobs felt like a chore. When you occupy your hands, you free your mind. You break the chains that bind and restrain your thoughts as you busy yourself with the task in front of you. Art is the best example of this, but many kinds of work are capable of achieving this mental freedom. It just depends on how strict the standards of production are for the task at hand.

While I was at Trilogy House, returning to college and finishing my education was talked about regularly between my parents and the doctor. I was more interested in publishing River Class and living the life of a best-selling author. I was mentally stable, but I still had my pipe dreams. To satisfy my parents, I agreed to go back to school. I enrolled in community college sometime in late 2011. As the seasonal landscaping job ended, and I found plenty of time on my hands, I began looking forward to returning to class. I was just going to school part time. I had algebra at 8:00 AM, and economics at 9:00 AM. The work load was lighter than taking 18 credits at a university, and I welcomed that. I also welcomed the intellectual stimulation. There wasn't much thought provoking activity in the past few months. Since May it felt like I had been massaging a corpse. There wasn't much effect. I completed my assignments with focus and confidence, and it felt rewarding. It all made sense even though I couldn't manage to stay awake during class without a cup of coffee. I sat in the front in an attempt to amplify my interest. It didn't work. It only made me more noticeable when my head leaned back, and my eyes went shut. We had to write a term paper for economics, and I picked the auto industry for my topic. In my research I found an eye-opener: the demand for luxury SUV's. The purchase of such a vehicle is the capitalist equivalent of masturbation. It's a feel-good-now kind of motion. It has little utility. I finished the semester with a B+ in algebra and an A in economics. It felt good get my mind in action again. This was the first semester of college I had completed without using drugs. I was impressed with my level of understanding. There were no mind blowing revelations, just a calm, consistent learning curve. My semester at community college was kind of a trial run to see if I could produce. I succeeded and I enrolled at the University of Pittsburgh at Johnstown for the following fall.

Classes were over for the time being, and summer was upon us. I went back to work for the landscaping company four days a week. Business had been on the decline for a few years and we didn't have the customer base to keep all crews busy 40+ a week. After the previous summer, I was happy to simply be working. Cheat Fest came and I attended it with some of the Johnstown paddling crew. I was grateful for the camaraderie. The Saturday sunrise was hidden by cloud cover. The skies were grey and the river was high. A friend offered me his river-runner to paddle. I was tempted. It was the boat that I learned to kayak in. As we dicked around that morning, I grew less and less interested in paddling. Drinking beer and listening to bluegrass music seemed more interesting. That's exactly what I did: drank beer and listened to bluegrass. I had fun. I had my friends, and I had my sanity.

Two weeks later was the Stonycreek Rendezvous. I borrowed the river-runner, and ran the Stony with three guys from high-school. One swam a lot. He was banged up, and exhausted by the time we got off the river. It was a good day though. I got to reconnect with a few people who had been out of my life for a little while, people who were once my closest friends. I was getting back to normal. I didn't have much of a taste for adventure from being medicated and institutionalized. I was turning into a bum, but the spirit of my friends fired up humor and a taste for adventure. Life was exciting again. That day, Stonycreek was a catalyst. Without it I may have remained bland and grey forever.

Nothing exciting happened that night, but I'll never forget the way I woke up the next morning. I laid sleeping in my tent when I heard the roar of an engine. My tent crashed in around me, and I felt an immense pressure on my chest as I opened my eyes.

"What a terrible dream!" I thought. Then the engine revved again, and I felt the weight of the pick-up truck on top of me once more. "This is no dream!" I thought as I wrestled about trying to get out of the collapsed tent.

"You're running somebody over!" I heard a man yell

"Thank God this was finally over!" I thought. I crawled out of the tent and saw my friends Nissan Frontier parked to the rear of my tent. I was fighting for my life without even seeing it coming. I was still half asleep as I wrestled with the collapsed tent. I barely had time to panic as I heard the engine roar and felt the truck on top of me. Surprise was about all I felt. The guy turned off the engine, and stepped out with a wide-eyed look of fear upon his face. "Are you okay!?" He asked. Nothing felt broke and my breathing was fine. There was a doctor in camp, and he came over and put his stethoscope to my chest. I felt fine once the truck was finished running me over. The driver couldn't see behind him. He had kayaks in the back of his truck blocking the view of my tent sitting 10 feet behind him. He jumped in the driver seat hung over without ever taking a glance at what was behind him, and threw the transmission in reverse. He said he felt some resistance then a bump. That was me. He didn't know what was in his way so he threw it in drive, and pulled forward across me a second time. He apologized whole-heartedly. He couldn't believe what he had done. He was just happy I was alive.

I went home Sunday morning, and laid on the couch for a while. I was a little sore, but generally okay. After about 2 hours, I got a phone call. It was my friend who had run me over. "Hey, the guys in Benscreek Canoe Club are pretty adamant about you going to the hospital." I told him that's fine, but I don't feel like driving. I figured he could give me a ride down since he *did* run me over just a few hours earlier. "I can take you," he said. "I'll be over in half an hour." We went to the emergency room, and they gave me an MRI and checked my urine. Everything came back fine, and I considered calling off work the next day. I didn't, but after running wheelbarrows full of mulch for a few hours Monday morning, I began to get sore. In a few days the soreness went away, and I was just left with a bad memory. It's a hard-and-fast joke in the Johnstown paddling community now. "Hey, guy, you run anybody over lately?" We laugh about it, but I often think of how lucky I was. Another foot to the left and the truck would have went over my head or neck. Who knows what would have happened then. All is well that ends well, or so they say. Sometimes I disagree on account of the shear anxiety bad memories create. I'm alive. That's all I really know.

Landscaping was putting some cash in my pocket, and keeping me busy through May and June, but I hated it. Towards the end of June I got a phone call from the owner of a local gas station offering me a job. I took it. I was in constant contact with customers and it demanded clear communication. My social skills improved immediately out of necessity. That was because of two reasons. One reason was the nature of the work, the other was the relationships with the coworkers. Every shift had two cashiers working, and there was usually a deli-worker in the kitchen. All but one of the employees who worked out front were younger than 35. I was one of the older ones, and undoubtedly the most eccentric. I usually worked Friday night, Saturday night, and Sunday morning. My shifts were paired with the same group of people, and one of the young ladies I regularly worked with said to me, "You're strange. You won't say anything for a while, then when you open your mouth, its like 'Holy shit, I can't believe you just said that!'" I kept people laughing. I was in recovery and nothing felt too serious. Everything about my life and the people in it was light and laughable.

The most tenured worker at the joint took a liking to me almost immediately. Most of the workers had a short temper with him, but I had patience. I listened to what he had to say, and socialized with him. When we were closing the store one night, he said to me "I like you. I can have a real conversation with you because you actually listen. You don't try to argue. You listen, and then you respond." The conversation that night was about creation and evolution. He argued on the side of creation, and I tried to explain to him my ideas about how they are one in the same. We enjoyed the debate. We listened and waited each our turns to talk. At the end of the night we both felt good about the conversation and were thankful for the opportunity to stand our point of views. That might be the most important standard for making an impact on people, on small scales and large: Be quick to listen, slow to speak, and slow to anger.

We had lots of fun working at the gas station. We talked about wild schemes, fantasies, and crazy ideas. Everyone kept everyone else laughing, and the only time it felt like work was when you had to wake up at 3:30 in the morning to open the store. The owner would raise his voice or get a short temper with the workers every once in a while, but he was harmless. He was talking to a new employee once, and said "I might yell, but that doesn't mean I'm angry with you." I overheard the conversation and piped up, "Yeah he's like one of those little ankle-biter dogs, he might bark a lot, but his bite's harmless." When the owner heard those words, he got a good laugh. He went around telling people that joke for months. Workers came and went pretty quickly. Most people through the revolving door were high school students looking for after-school, and summer jobs.

Almost a year after I started working there, we hired a kid about 3 years younger than me. We didn't really cross paths until a few of us went out for beers one night. The two of us were standing outside the bar smoking cigarettes, and the moment began with an awkward silence. I could tell he was a little guarded. He was smaller in stature, and rode with the counter-culture in high school. I just started talking about something useless and stupid, and the conversation evolved into something interesting, and thought provoking. I made a new friend. My buddy, who is now one of my closest friends, kind of struck me as a nerdy hipster. He was a wry little shit. We'll call him Jesse. Quick witted, Jesse's genuine personality and abrasive sense of humor made me like him immediately despite how nerdy he was. I invited him to the bar next time I went out, and music was the backbone of the conversation. Jesse played drums, and when he found out I played bass, we tried to organize a jam. "We need a guitarist," I said. "I know a guy" was his reply. About a week before we were set to rock out, I bumped into a dude at a party. We'll call him Jim. I was drinking my beer at a pig-roast, and I could hear Jim talking, loud, head-strong, funny. "I gotta meet this guy," I thought. I introduced myself. When we found out each other played music, naturally, we organized a jam. Little did I know, that Jim was the guy Jesse had in mind. There was chemistry there. All three of us were kind of nuts, Jim and I more so than Jesse, but he's no average Joe, either. Its been said that he goes there.

It was the end of July in 2013 when we showed up at Jim's apartment in a rough section of Johnstown. I had my bass and amp in the back of the Subaru. Jesse sat in the passenger seat, with his drum set waiting in a basement across town. Jim loaded his guitar and amp into my car and we high-tailed it across town. We arrived to an empty house around 7 in the evening, walked downstairs, and began setting things up. The lighting was shitty. Water was pooling on the floor, and the ceiling was a little low for my height. We were cramped into a dungeon. We plugged in, tuned up, and rocked out. Jesse was poundin' some groovy beats, I ate them up, and sweated out something bluesy. Jim read me, and shredded something grungy on the 1-4-5's. The dark squalor of the basement brought soul to the three of us. We rocked heavy. The beats were loud and thick. We sweated with music in the wet, dark basement as we pounded and blasted our instruments in rockin' harmony. We jammed for about two hours, sweating our asses off and playing out our souls and minds, absorbing and exalting it, all at the same time. We went on feeling the vibrations until about 9:30, then I cracked. "I need a cigarette," I admitted, and everyone else agreed. We stood in the alley behind the house, burning fags, and I asked Jim,

"Got anything left?"

"Nah," he replied. I was spent as well, but off in some euphoric land as we finished our smokes, and packed up our gear. It was raw, and Earth-shattering. It felt primal. It was the first time in a long time. The power of the music was new, original, and hand crafted on the spot. I felt alive, throbbing with excitement as our vibrations broke the glass and released the fluid of rock and roll. The sweat on our bodies and release in our minds was conformation that we were giving the beats our all. *This was the reason for living.*

Chapter 13: Spirits

A Year later I was at a party drinking beer and playing guitar around a fire near a house back in the woods. There were a few pretentious and self-indulged people invited and one of them kept spatting off at the mouth dramatically. My temper ran short. My mouth got away from me under a haze of reefer, and I began cutting down the rude minority. I could hear myself talk, but I had no control of what I was saying. The words came out much more passive-aggressively than they usually do, and I felt strange about it. It was self-righteous, but I took a look at what I was doing, and what I was saying. I tried to humbled myself in regret as I stood there. As I stepped back to take an introspective glance, I thought about how fragile life is, and how challenging living can be. I looked at myself and saw the connections between my consciousness, and the people and places I have been, and where I was at that moment.

Most of the beer had been drank and everyone else had already left or crawled into their tents for the night. The half-acre yard on the hillside, enclosed by woods, was empty. I was the only one up, sitting around the large fireplace with a big flame burning in the middle. I looked at my cigarette and thought, "I'm going to bed as soon as I'm done with this." I looked at the fire once more, then looked up, and saw a man sitting across from me. The fire illuminated his white robe, long dark hair, and his beard. The man wasn't sitting there a second ago. It was an apparition. I was surprised and awe-struck. I studied the strangely familiar face for a second as he sat across from me, silently, without expression on his face. I was creeped out. I had a tough time believing what I was seeing. By the time I accepted that I was sitting around a fire with the risen spirit of Jesus Christ, he had vanished. In that moment, I was baptized in the Holy Spirit according to Christian elders. I looked around for clues, and comfort, but all I saw was the dark woods, and as my eyes combed through the trees, I could hear the wind whisper the words "The Holy Spirit" around me. I was not joyful, I was not at peace. I was rattled, and uneasy about the whole situation. I was in disbelief.

As I thought about the moment over, and over again, I accepted what I had seen and heard. My encounter with Jesus that night alone around the fire branded the infinite power of the Holy Spirit into my mind. I only shared this encounter with four other people. I know how unlikely the story sounds, but more powerful things have happened without explanation. Why me? I asked. Like so many other times, the only answer I could muster was "Because it is." Life on the brink of death, schizophrenia, love, hate, betrayal, maybe it all needed an exclamation point. I had gone on trial, and resurrected my soul. Christ came to me that night to destroy any doubts I may have about my faith in the future. Maybe the novelty of success would wear off, and the excitement would die down, and I would become one of the proud, self-indulged individuals. Whatever the reason, no one can ever make me believe that my God, Christ, and the Holy Spirit were not with me that night.

That night made me think about the sacrifices Jesus made for the sake of every man's, woman's, and child's soul. Two weeks later, my pastor baptized me with water in a lake nearby. I stood at the water's edge and the pastor called me into the lake. He asked if I denounce evil and believe in Jesus Christ, then he drew me backwards below the surface of the water three times. It was a jubilant moment of reckoning that liberated me in the steadfast knowledge of my eternal salvation.

Chapter 14: Peace

In 2014 I graduated Pitt-Johnstown with a Bachelor of Science degree in Geology, and began working for the state government in environmental protection. That year wasn't a dull hum. I was working hard to make sure all the perseverance in the past three years did not fall short of accomplishing my goals, and distancing myself from a painful youth. Fast living put me in bad places, and I had to make sacrifices to move past all the painful memories and hard situations in life. Getting a job as a cashier at a gas station was a good move once I became mentally stable. I made new friends because of it, and was able to express humor day in and day out. That became important when I was wrapping up college. The geology program was a tight-knit cohort of students, and I was the center of attention a lot of the time. Our summer semester of field methods was a testimony to that. My sense of adventure, and thirst for exploration spilled over to the other students as we did our field work, and made each other laugh and scratch our heads. The whole class went on a camping trip once, and I was by far the most intoxicated that night. A few years of regularing dive bars in Johnstown built a drinker out of me. In all honesty the urge to get down and party never left. It was only suppressed for a short period of time. I didn't forget who I was or what made me smile, and that's important. Everyone has an identity. It comes from the values you hold close to your heart. It is built out of the relationships you hold with the people and world around you. For me, finding faith, and building a relationship with God has given me an identity that I can take satisfaction in. Resiliency might be the one word that could sum up my young life, but it did not come without the Great Spirit. I call on God for strength and comfort often, and He delivers me. It is crucial not to disconnect from the world and people around you just because you face a time of dullness or adversity. It's hard to achieve success and be happy, but through God, I continue to find ways, time and again. The support I had from friends and family was no shortcoming, either. I doubt I would have been able to do it without them. Without them I would have been a delinquent. Now I work in the outdoors, and get to spend plenty of time doing the things I love. I am not happy all the time, but I look forward to good possibilities, and make the sacrifices to live a happy life. No heavy drug-use. No detachment from faith, friends, family, or doctors. And things like meditation, physical exercise, prayer, and worship help anxiety and depression. At the very least, they give me something to look forward to that cost nothing more than a little drive and motivation. And writing. I never lost the desire to share my thoughts and experiences with people. Maybe I just do it out of habit, but something tells me that people like to hear the things I have to say. I have been given the ability to share insight in interesting ways, so part of me feels a duty to keep the keys cracking. But most importantly, I never lost the determination to keep my connection with the people, places, and things that build my identity. A campfire in the mountains on a warm night with friendly faces, and a pipe full of smoke keeps my heart warm. I want my heart to stay warm all the way until the very end.

Made in the USA
Monee, IL
12 April 2024

56464169R00073